KU-541-918

AUTISTIC SPECTRUM DISORDER:

Positive Approaches for Teaching Children with ASD

by
DIANA SEACH

A NASEN Publication

Published in 1998

© Diana Seach

All rights reserved. No part of this publication may be reproduced or transmitted in any form
or by any means, electronic, mechanical, photocopying, recording, or otherwise without the
prior permission of the publishers.

ISBN 1 901485 01 3

The right of the author to be identified as author of this work has been asserted by her in
accordance with the Copyright, Designs and Patents Act 1988.

Published by NASEN.
NASEN is a registered charity. Charity No. 1007023.
NASEN is a company limited by guarantee, registered in England and Wales.
Company No. 2674379.

BRIDGEND COLLEGE LIBRARY

CLASS No. 371.94 SEA

COPY 00022181   PRICE £10.00

O. 76019
REQ. (NASEN)   DATE 4/07/2000
R.21922

Further copies of this book and details of NASEN's many other publications may be obtained
from the Publications Department at its registered office:
NASEN House, 4/5, Amber Business Village, Amber Close, Amington, Tamworth, Staffs., B77 4RP.
Tel: 01827 311500 Fax: 01827 313005
Email: welcome@nasen.org.uk

Cover design by Graphic Images.
Typeset in Palatino by J. C. Typesetting.
Printed in the United Kingdom by Stowes (Stoke-on-Trent).

AUTISTIC SPECTRUM DISORDER:

Positive Approaches for Teaching Children with ASD

Contents

Acknowledgements

The author wishes to thank:
Sarah Cooper, Jonathan Fogell, Peter Gordon, Anna Leesley, Bob Rendall, Lesley Strickland, Lorna Wing and parents and pupils of Fordwater School, Chichester.

AUTISTIC SPECTRUM DISORDER:

Positive Approaches for Teaching Children with ASD

Preface

This book provides an introduction to the nature of the autistic disorder. It will be of use to anyone currently working with children within the autistic spectrum in a specialist setting, or where there are plans for children with this disorder to be integrated into another learning environment. In addition to information about diagnosis and assessment, it also identifies some positive strategies which may be helpful when working in the classroom with children who have autistic spectrum disorder. The book also includes a chapter on some of the approaches which have been developed to support children with an autistic disorder. They describe different therapeutic or interactive methods which can be adapted for working with the child in the home or at school.

AUTISTIC SPECTRUM DISORDER (ASD) is the generic term used in the diagnosis of people who have autism or autistic type behaviours and includes those with severe learning difficulties and those who have above average intelligence (Wing, 1996). The complex nature of the disorder has led to much debate amongst educationalists and the medical professions because the range of features associated with the disorder can vary between individuals and can be identified in children with other mental or physical disabilities.

Following Kanners' identification of the disorder in 1943, autism was for many years thought to be the result of a psychosocial disturbance affecting behaviour and treatment was based on psychotherapy and behaviour modification. Research since the 1960s has played an important role in identifying a number of causal factors affecting brain function and has helped to provide explanations for the range of features associated with the disorder (Lotter, 1974; Wing, 1976; Rutter, 1971, 1972; Rutter and Schopler, 1978). Consequently there has been a move to adopt different methods of teaching which include a consideration of the child's developmental level and his or her individual differences.

Whilst all children with ASD have a right to access the National Curriculum, some may require considerable support with personal and social communication skills to enable them to participate more effectively within their learning environment. The majority of children with ASD will have a placement where they will have access to a curriculum suited to their developmental level, while a small minority will be educated in schools specifically for children with ASD. Some severely affected children with additional psychological problems, may require a more specialised therapeutic environment which will incorporate their educational programme.

Meeting the needs of children with special educational needs has broad implications for local education authorities in terms of resourcing, training and provision. By recognising the various levels of need, local education authorities are having to look at the variations in provision which best reflect and promote common recognition of the continuum of special educational needs (Code of Practice, DfEE, 1994).

This model of practice is particularly relevant when considering the education of children with ASD. Because of the broad spectrum of ability associated with this disorder, children will be found in a variety of different educational establishments which will include mainstream and special schools. Subsequently there are significant variations not only in the type of provision available but in the teaching approaches used to support children's learning. A teaching style which is appropriate for other children, with or without learning difficulties, may fail to engage a child with ASD because of the level of social and communication difficulties they are experiencing.

It is widely acknowledged that the co-operation between different agencies and partnership with parents is essential in planning the education of children with special educational needs. Information on the various organisations and voluntary bodies involved in education and support for children with ASD has therefore been included.

CHAPTER 1
What Is Autistic Spectrum Disorder?

Autism has been described as a disability affecting the development of communication and social interaction. It is also characterised by the rigid behaviours which individuals display because of a lack of flexibility in their thought processes.

History

Kanner (1943) identified a group of children who were suffering from an *autistic aloneness* which had a profound effect on all behaviour. This included how they appeared to relate better to objects rather than people and had an anxious desire for sameness. He also acknowledged that some of these children had 'islets of ability' and were able to recall events and sequences with remarkable skill. In terms of language development he also recognised that many children remained mute and for those that did develop speech, the language used was often not intended for interpersonal communication.

The following year Asperger (1944) wrote a paper about a group of children who had fundamental difficulties with communication and social integration resulting in what he described as a *disturbance of contact*, but they had a normal or above average intelligence. Whilst the children appeared to have a good acquisition of language and a fascination for verbal usage they still had fundamental problems with the social aspects of language. Due to the pronounced lack of flexibility they also had a narrow range of interests and specific rituals to adhere to, similar to those that Kanner identified. It was also noted that they had a tendency to be ill-coordinated and had poor physical and visual-motor skills.

Those with Asperger syndrome can also experience anxiety attacks and become withdrawn because there is a heightened awareness of being misunderstood and not understanding others. This can also develop from not feeling able to fit in socially. Asperger syndrome is now considered to be one of the disorders within the autistic spectrum (Wing, 1996).

Aetiology of the Disorder

Although no single cause has been identified for the disorder there is a significant genetic component which has been found (Folstein & Rutter, 1977). Autism was considered to be a psychogenic disorder (Bettelheim, 1967) and in some instances the term 'childhood schizophrenia' was also used. This definition has largely been refuted since research has shown that the language delay, the poor social skills and the repetitive and ritualistic behaviours are the result of brain dysfunction (Rutter et al, 1971). The recognition of an organic basis for the disorder not only accounts for the range of features associated with autism but provides an explanation for the variations in the severity of the disorder (Frith, 1989).

The psychological and pathological explanations for ASD include the following:

  genetic disorder
  metabolic disorder
  chromosome abnormality
  immune dysfunction
  birth trauma
  premature birth
  brain injury

In Folstein and Rutter's twin studies (1977) they found a high percentage amongst monozygotic twins where one child had autism or some other language or cognitive disability. Further studies of siblings (August et al, 1983) have found many families where a sibling had a related disability such as a language disorder or specific learning disability (dyslexia).

Autism has also been found in those with tuberous sclerosis, a genetic disorder, and in those with the chromosome abnormality, Fragile X. Phenylketonuria (PKU), an inherited metabolic disorder, has been associated with autism, if left untreated. Those affected by other physical disorders such as infantile spasms and maternal rubella may also show features of the disorder.

In some cases young children who had a high fever illness, such as meningitis or encephalitis, developed a late onset of autism as have some children who have been exposed to high doses of antibiotics following an illness. There is also the question as to whether some children have been affected after having the MMR vaccination. The yeast infection, candida albicans, has also been linked with some children who have ASD and current research by Shattock et al (1997) relates certain bowel disorders to autism. All of these examples of late onset suggest that there may be evidence of brain chemical abnormalities, with the illness or medication acting as a trigger for the emergence of the autism. Autism can also be found in children with other mental or physical disabilities such as Down's syndrome, Rett's syndrome, Angelman's syndrome, cerebral palsy and epilepsy.

The estimated prevalence rate of autistic spectrum disorder, which includes those with Asperger syndrome, affects 56 per 10,000 of the population and affects four times as many boys as girls (National Autistic Society, 1995). All those with an autistic spectrum disorder will display the Triad of Impairments.

The Triad of Impairments

The Triad of Impairments (Wing & Gould, 1979) is now recognised as a diagnosis for autistic spectrum disorder by the World Health Organisation's register, the International Classification of Diseases, ICD-10 and the American Register of Psychiatric Disorders, the Diagnostic and Statistical Manual of Mental Disorders, DSM-1V.

The Triad of Impairments consists of:

> an impairment in social interaction
> an impairment in social communication
> an impairment in thought and imagination

Social Interaction

There is a fundamental disability in developing social empathy usually characterised by difficulties in understanding the feelings and behaviour of others. Consequently, individuals may be very withdrawn and make little attempt at social contact except to have their needs met. This impairment in social interaction has been described as 'aloof'.

Wing and Gould also recognised children who were very 'passive' and compliant and who rarely made spontaneous approaches towards others. There were also those who behaved in ways which have been described as 'odd', such as using an inappropriate greeting, touching clothing or being aggressive.

They may have difficulty understanding that different social situations require different social behaviours and consequently some of their responses can be asocial. Certain social contexts may also cause them distress or confusion because of the social demands of the situation.

Social Communication

An impairment in communication includes a difficulty in making sense of and using all aspects of verbal and non-verbal communication. Many children never develop speech, not because they do not have the mechanics for the development of language but because they are not using it as a tool for communication. There can be a significant language delay which, when it does

5

appear, may be very repetitive, learned phrases (especially from TV adverts!) or echolalic (echoed speech). Consequently there are significant pragmatic language difficulties because of the ways in which they attempt to use communication.

Some children who appear to have a good expressive use of language may still have difficulties understanding meanings as they tend to interpret information very literally. They may focus on a particular topic which interests them and talk about it to someone without realising what a conversation involves.

Another aspect of the impairment is that language can be very context bound and where they may be able to use language in one situation they may not be able to in another. Difficulties with communication can extend to other areas such as gesture, facial expression, eye contact and body language where they may not be able to interpret these additional cues and consequently miss the point of what they are being asked to do.

Thought and Imagination

An impairment in thought and imagination extends to every area of their thinking, language and behaviour. The repetitive and obsessive behaviours can dominate their daily activities and have profound effects on their family and those who work with them. Changes in routines can cause the child distress because they are dependent on routines as a way of understanding their environment. They like to keep to special rituals, often having a very limited diet because they will only eat certain foods, or taking the same routes when they go out in the car. It is probably this aspect of the disorder which most profoundly affects how children with ASD are managed both at home and in school.

In the early identification of the disorder, an impairment with play and imaginative activities is very noticeable. Children and even young babies may be fixated on a particular toy or they may play with it in a certain way, for example spinning the wheels of a car rather than pushing it along. They will also tend to be more interested in objects rather than people and either seek out things which fascinate them or make collections of them. Some obsessions may always remain with them whilst others will change. Some children may develop an interest in a particular topic which they will want to talk or read about constantly, anything from air vents to earthquakes!

Additional Features

In addition to the Triad of Impairments there are a number of secondary features which will also affect some children and these will have a profound effect on how they respond to their learning environment. Consideration should also be given to these when planning their educational provision and an individual education plan.

- Hand flapping or other repetitious movements such as spinning, rocking or jumping

These activities may occur when they are anxious but can also be self-stimulatory. Unfortunately these mannerisms can draw attention to the child.

- Abnormal responses to sensory information including sound, smell, taste, touch or visual stimuli

These can significantly impair the child's ability to attend to a particular task or interpret information in an environment which has too much auditory or visual stimulation. Certain stimuli can cause distress or fascination, so careful consideration will have to be given to individual responses.

- Erratic sleeping or eating patterns

These can severely disrupt the management of the child in the home but also have implications for how they function in school. Additional support at home with a programme to modify the difficulties may help when the child is young so that these problems do not continue into later life.

- Self-injurious or aggressive behaviour

These can occur in children who are more severely affected or suffering from some additional psychological disturbance. Aggressive behaviour is often a response to frustration and confusion which can be heightened for those who have poor language skills. Children who self-injure may be doing so because of localised pain which they are unable to communicate to others.

- Hyperactivity

This can affect children's ability to concentrate and attend for a specific length of time on a particular activity. It may require a very structured learning programme to modify the behaviour or some medical intervention, depending on the underlying cause.

- Poor motor coordination, a strange gait or posture

Whilst many may show a remarkable agility and be very adept at some fine motor skills, there are those who have significant difficulties with motor coordination and may find hand/eye exercises particularly difficult. It may also be that these children adopt such postures which are compensating for their lack of understanding of social behaviour and reflect their impaired view of the self. Children with Asperger syndrome may also be prone to clumsiness which can be a source of ridicule by their peers. Programmes of physical education and movement integration are beneficial for correcting difficulties in motor control.

- Irrational fears and phobias

In addition to anxieties children may show in social situations, they may also have severe reactions to certain stimuli which can give rise to an emotional response. This reaction is understandable where the child may not have the verbal skills to express their concerns. It will be important that those working with them are aware of things that may trigger abnormal reactions by removing the object or experience likely to cause distress.

- A special creative or mathematical skill

About 10% of people with ASD will have a particular skill in music, art, remembering dates or making complicated mathematical calculations (National Autistic Society, 1995). These are what Kanner called 'islets of ability' and the term 'idiot savant' has occasionally been used to describe those who clearly have difficulties in social communication and yet have a remarkable cognitive skill.

CHAPTER 2

The Learning Difficulties of Pupils with Autistic Spectrum Disorder

Having established that children with ASD will have difficulties in the areas of communication, social interaction and in the way they think and process information, what implications does this have for how they learn?

Education is about communicating information and sharing ideas and learning is a consequence of this experience. If these two aspects of learning are fundamentally impaired, the ways in which a child is taught will require a much more child-centred approach.

It is important to recognise that although children with ASD will have the same core impairments, there is not one pattern of learning and teaching which works for every child. What helps one child with ASD may not be suitable for another and their own response to learning will be as varied as it is for any child.

For most children their routes to learning and acquiring skills will be markedly different to those of their peers. One reason for this is that they have an inconsistent developmental profile and may learn a skill without having previously understood the concepts normally required to achieve it. This is an important feature and one which is fundamental to the teaching of children with ASD.

One child I taught spoke only in echolalic phrases and had no spontaneous speech except 'yes' and 'no' which he used to answer questions. Recognising that he was very skilled at the visual recognition of symbols, I introduced words which he soon memorised. It then became evident that by teaching him to read he was gaining an understanding of the use of speech through prose. Gradually he was using more spontaneous phrases and sentences and initiating conversations which also helped to improve his skills in social interaction.

Positive strategies for teaching children with ASD focus on the compensating abilities of each individual whilst acknowledging those aspects of learning where they are having difficulty. Although these can vary depending on the severity of the disorder it is important to remember that because the autistic spectrum covers the full range of intellectual ability, there will be some similarities which those with ASD share with their peers as well as those areas where they can excel beyond their peer level, such as logical and spatial tasks.

Difficulty	Compensating Ability
short-term memory	long-term memory
attention	focus on interests
problem solving	not easily bored
generalising	skills they can use
symbolic play	functional recognition
social isolation	independent behaviour
motivation and self-image	activities which interest them
language	good visual and spatial skills

Memory

Memory is an area where children with ASD may show considerable skill. They may be able to recall 'lists' and 'chunks of information' based on visual details or episodes which are stored as visual facts. For one non verbal child one example of her long-term memory skill included knowing the route to the house of a relation whom they had not seen for several years and when they arrived went to a room to look for the same toy they had played with when they last visited.

Where children with ASD can have difficulty is with the short-term memory and the problem of performing a task they have just been set or remembering a story they have just been told.

This may be due to too much verbal information being given which they are then not able to process and take in the important details. One useful strategy could be to write down a list of what they need to do or represent it in pictures. This can help them to concentrate on the task rather than worry because they have not understood what they were asked to do.

Attention

The problems of attention in children with ASD can be described as a difficulty with over-stimulation. Here the child may react either to a specific object or to too much information within the environment. If the task a child has been set is not meaningful to them it will not hold as much interest to them as, for example, the way the dust falls where the sun is shining through the window. It may be worth considering where the child sits in the classroom so that any distractions from light or noise are reduced.

A fascination with visual stimuli can also be one way of bringing the child's attention to a particular activity, for example if the child is 'twiddling' a brick, other bricks can be introduced to show the child how to build a tower.

Baron-Cohen (1989) has identified that many young children with ASD are impaired in their use of pointing, a gesture which involves shared attention with another person. On the one hand, children are able to use a pointing gesture to gain a desired object, or indeed take the adult's hand to something they want, but then they do less well at tasks which involve the child inviting another person to share in what they are seeing, such as pointing to an aeroplane in the sky.

Problem Solving

Problem solving can pose difficulties for many children with ASD because they are dependent upon a set of strategies or learned responses to cope with a particular situation. It can also give rise to anxiety or confusion if a rule they have learnt in one situation does not work in another. Equally, the child who has poor understanding of social behaviour may have a problem working out how they should behave towards different people.

Where other children may become easily bored by doing the same activity in a particular situation, children with ASD may be happy with the routine of the same task because it is something they can do and they understand what is required. If one child in the class always likes to do the washing up it is quite likely that the other children in the class will not mind at all!

Through the curriculum, children with ASD will be given many situations in which to increase their range of experiences and with appropriate support can be helped to develop strategies for solving problems. Since they are unlikely to achieve this through incidental learning, staff working with the child can make use of things the child can do or enjoys doing so that he or she is more motivated to learn.

Generalising

The ability to generalise skills they have learnt poses problems for many children with ASD. They may have learnt a particular skill in one context but then have difficulty retrieving the knowledge they have learnt, in another situation. This can relate to their difficulties with language as well their thought processing. Making a cup of tea in the school kitchen may be one independence skill the child is being taught but at home where the cups are in a different place or the teapot is a different colour such subtle differences can affect how well he or she can manage.

Ensuring that a lot of over-learning takes place can help the child to understand the task so that they can achieve more independence skills. If the task involved has an element of practical application it will be easier for them to transfer skills. If they are always having to be reliant upon verbal or written instructions they may be more confused about what they have to do.

Teaching functional daily tasks in context is one way in which they can be helped to understand a particular skill they will need. Learning about using money by going shopping is likely to be more relevant to them than only completing sums and money recognition tasks in class.

Symbolic Play

Symbolic play is often seen as a vital component of language and cognitive development and is an area in young children with autism which can be significantly impaired. Leslie (1987) described this difficulty with pretend play to be fundamental to the Triad of Impairments since he feels it explains why people with ASD have impaired social relationships. He also recognises that a lack of semantic understanding or seeing one object as representing another also contributes to the impairments in communication. Consequently many children do not necessarily pick up on using a toy in a way that is not repetitive, for example lining them up or only playing with toys that are the same colour. In the absence of symbolic play, the development of language can be equally as effective by encouraging the functional use of objects. After all, why put a cup to your mouth with a pretend drink of tea in it when just as much language and social interaction can happen in the real situation.

Social Isolation

The social isolation which marks much of the behaviour of children with ASD can be particularly difficult to manage especially in classes where there is only one child with this disability. The aloofness can often be a problem for others in the class and for the teacher attempting to involve the child in other class activities. It is not always the case that the child is showing a preference for being alone but in order to make sense of a particular task they are trying to block out the spoken language and contact with others to focus on their work.

There will be other aspects of their social behaviour which are unique to the individual and these can become more evident in the learning environment where previously they had not been a problem at home.

Baron-Cohen, Leslie and Frith (1985) have established a view that what children with ASD lack is a 'Theory of Mind', a recognition that others have minds and can have separate thoughts and feelings to their own. A failure to understand this will mean that a person would be unable to predict others' behaviour and have no idea about how their behaviour is affecting others. However, not all children with ASD can be said to lack an understanding of others' mental states. Some more able children with ASD may develop an understanding of inference or intention from someone's actions but it is likely that they will respond to it with the same learned behaviour. For those with better language skills, they can be taught strategies which can heighten their awareness in the ways they relate and respond towards others.

Rather than expecting the child with ASD to take part in every social activity, staff should recognise that they can work independently and therefore should be given opportunities to do so. It is possible to identify some subjects in the curriculum which are more appropriate for independent work than others. Children with ASD tend to learn a new skill better in a one-to-one situation rather than in a social group. This is because they can have difficulty coping with the demands of what they need to do at the same time as coping with the social contact and the language used.

Motivation and Self-Image

In children with ASD a lack of motivation and a poor self-image can be the consequence of not recognising the 'self' in relation to others. Children who have difficulty understanding the mental states of others will have problems interpreting what others are thinking and feeling and how their behaviour affects others. If the work set provides no motivation there will be little desire to succeed at it and consequently no opportunity to receive praise for what has been achieved. On the other hand, many children with ASD are motivated by their own ritualistic and obsessional behaviours and interests so these can be used to gain the children's attention and developed into topics of study. A child who can share something he or she is interested in with others in the class, may be more motivated to learn because of the contribution that he or she has made within the class. A positive response from others can be the key to children with ASD attempting other tasks or learning new skills.

For more severely affected children, they can be motivated through an activity which they enjoy such as swimming or music or using the computer, all of which can provide opportunities for language development and social interaction. Once again, the routine of doing a familiar activity can be more motivating than one that is constantly being changed and which makes them confused about what they are expected to do.

Language

The language difficulties of children with ASD will permeate into all aspects of their thinking and behaviour. Although not all children with ASD will have problems with language it is invariably the use of language for communication which presents them with the most difficulties. Often a competent speaker can mislead others into assuming that because speech production is adequate this is synonymous with understanding. As speech emerges there is a tendency for it to lack intonation and it can appear pedantic. The interpretation of language can also prove quite daunting in terms of recognising humour, sarcasm and politeness. One teacher was wanting to let her student know that she was pleased with the efforts he was making with his work by telling him he was trying hard. However, the concept of 'trying' was very difficult for him to understand.

Many children with ASD remain mute and they will be reliant upon an augmented system of communication appropriate to their level of understanding. Signing and the use of symbols and photographs have all been used to support children's language development. The imitation and use of signs can be difficult for some children because of the social implications attached to them. A child who has difficulty interpreting body language may have a problem trying to work out which hand movement is meant for communication and which is made as a spontaneous gesture. However, this is not to say that signs are not an effective communication system and they can be used in conjunction with other methods.

Children with ASD are very strong visual learners and they cope much better with the written word, picture, symbol or object than they do with the spoken word. A word, symbol, object of reference, or a photograph can provide a visual cue for an activity or help a child to sequence their work where they may have difficulty interpreting too much verbal information. In some instances children have been able to develop a symbols vocabulary which they can use in order to communicate with others, for example indicating that they need to use the toilet or making a choice about an activity. For those experiencing some visual impairment, their work will need to be supplemented either with instructions written in large print or by using the computer.

Conclusion

As in all aspects of learning there will be some children with ASD who, in an initial assessment, may not appear to be having particular problems in these areas. A child, for example, who is very attentive to every word the teacher is saying during a lesson may in fact be finding it difficult to separate the important pieces of information from the less important comments or examples. They may then have difficulty recalling the most relevant facts for a piece of work they are doing.

If a child is given a problem solving task relating to a subject that he or she is good at, such as mathematics, it may suggest that skills like logical interpretations could be transferred to other areas of learning. However, this may not be the case, especially in subjects which demand a higher level of social interaction and language understanding such as English or Science.

Many children with ASD, when observed, can appear to be playing with toys imaginatively. I have even observed a child playing 'mummies and daddies' with dolls in the playhouse but closer observation revealed that the pattern of play and the language used was always the same, with phrases and situations that the child had recognised at home. Intervention by an adult to change the story was met with consternation. Another child would hand me a play telephone to talk to his mum, but was never observed doing this himself.

Both the social difficulties and the language impairment can present with a whole range of competencies which can affect the level at which the child appears to be functioning. A greater emphasis placed on the use of the computer, pictures or symbols and the written word, are likely to help in developing more independent ways of learning.

It is also important to remember that every child with ASD, regardless of his or her learning difficulty, has a personality which will influence how he or she responds to the environment and learns new skills. Likewise how others treat them will affect how they feel about themselves and how they will learn in different social contexts.

CHAPTER 3
Identification and Assessment

Given the complex nature of the autistic disorder the process of identification and assessment can often be compounded by the different routes to diagnosis and the age at which this occurs. In the majority of cases the medical profession will have identified with the parents aspects of developmental delay by the time the child is 3 years old, although it can be earlier in some cases.

Medical Diagnosis
A diagnosis needs to be made as early as possible so that parents can obtain the appropriate support they need. It would also mean that when the child reaches school age, their learning difficulties will be understood in terms of the disorder and the teacher or special educational needs coordinator (SENCO) will be able to prepare an individual education plan which best reflects the needs and strengths of the child. If the nature of the child's disability is not recognised early enough, then this can have a profound effect on their potential for learning and management of their behaviour (Howlin & Rutter, 1987).

If there has been a medical diagnosis of the disorder before the child starts school then the process of assessments can begin much earlier and the child will benefit from an appropriate placement in a special or mainstream school. Schools will then have the responsibility of ensuring that resources are put in place to support a child with ASD and that staff are fully informed about the nature of the child's learning difficulty.

There are a number of professionals who will be involved with the parents in providing relevant information and assessments before a formal diagnosis is made. These will include:

> general practitioner
> health visitor
> community paediatrician
> consultant psychiatrist
> child and adolescent mental health services
> child development centres in hospitals
> teacher and/or SENCO
> physiotherapist
> speech and language therapist
> clinical psychologist
> educational psychologist
> social services

Information from any of these sources should give a clear picture of the nature of the child's learning needs, although not all children who display the Triad of Impairments will have a diagnosis of ASD. There are a number of reasons for this:

- There may be an associated learning disability, eg dual sensory impairment, Fragile X, Rett's syndrome, Tuberous Sclerosis, Angelmans' syndrome, epilepsy.
- Parents may be uncertain about the cause of the disorder.
- Professionals may not want to be seen 'labelling' a child's disability.
- Diagnostic procedures and assessments may take a number of years and for some, especially those with Asperger syndrome, diagnosis may not begin until they are in their teens or young adulthood.

A diagnosis of ASD will be made by a multi-professional team using a series of developmental, psychological and behavioural assessments. One problem here is that different interpretations can be given for the observed behaviours and the nature of the communication difficulties can be assessed under the guise of other language disorders rather than identifying the Triad of Impairments. Currently the lack of a standardised diagnostic process has highlighted the need for a more cohesive assessment procedure made by those in the medical profession who have a sound knowledge of the disorder.

Some of the ways in which diagnosis is made are indicated in the figures below. These routes to diagnosis can of course vary in different parts of the country but most children will be seen initially by a member of the medical profession, either a GP or a health visitor. In some instances parents may go directly to a specialist diagnostic unit following a referral by a fund-holding GP.

The Different Routes to Diagnosis

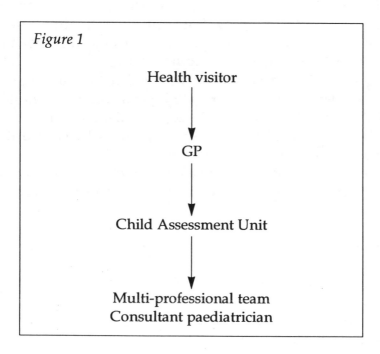

Figure 1

Health visitor

↓

GP

↓

Child Assessment Unit

↓

Multi-professional team
Consultant paediatrician

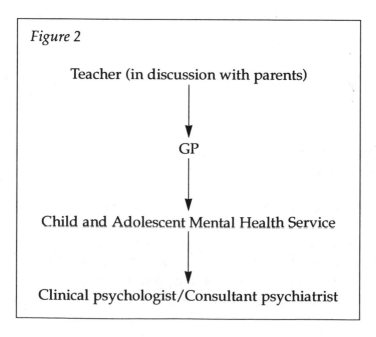

Figure 2

Teacher (in discussion with parents)

↓

GP

↓

Child and Adolescent Mental Health Service

↓

Clinical psychologist/Consultant psychiatrist

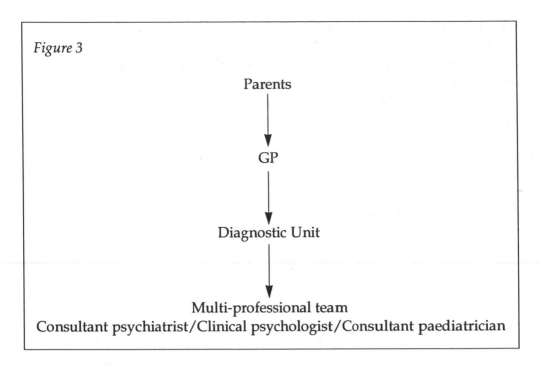

Figure 3

Parents

↓

GP

↓

Diagnostic Unit

↓

Multi-professional team
Consultant psychiatrist/Clinical psychologist/Consultant paediatrician

In many cases, the words 'autism', 'autistic spectrum disorder' or 'Asperger syndrome' do not appear in medical or psychological assessments or subsequently in a Statement of special educational needs as an explanation for the child's learning difficulty. Instead, the terminology used suggests a feature of the disorder. This can be misleading especially as these difficulties can occur in children where autism is not present. The following may be referred to:

challenging behaviour
attention deficit/hyperactive disorder (ADHD)
semantic/pragmatic difficulties
hyperactivity
obsessive/compulsive disorder
emotional and behaviour difficulties
developmental delay
global retardation
language disorder
epilepsy
social and communication difficulties

Pervasive Developmental Disorder (PDD) is the diagnostic term used in the USA to describe the whole spectrum of autism and atypical autistic disorders. Whilst it is similar to the Triad of Impairments it is yet another label which may cause further confusion in terms of a diagnosis.

School-based Assessment
Where a formal diagnosis has not been made prior to the child starting school it may fall to the teacher, headteacher or SENCO to begin discussions with parents about aspects of learning which have been identified as problem areas for a particular child.

Within the classroom environment teachers will soon become aware of the child who is not responding in the same way as their peers.

The following are some examples:

- does not appear to want social contact and may react adversely when others approach;
- is not readily able to understand the social meanings and inferences involved in communication;

15

- may have difficulty concentrating and sitting still;
- panics about work not being done correctly;
- misses the point of conversations and games and becomes an object of ridicule;
- is over-concerned about following rules and instructions;
- becomes aggressive or displays attention-seeking behaviour when anxious;
- is not able to keep up with the pace of work required;
- will not show any regard for the emotions and feelings of others;
- talks about an obsessional interest constantly and does not accept a change of topic easily.

Some LEAs may also have their own policies on the identification and assessment of children with special educational needs and these should be consulted before any assessments take place.

What Type of Assessment

Where there has not been a clear diagnosis of an autistic spectrum disorder teachers may find it more relevant to follow an assessment which is autism specific. Aarons and Gittens (1992) have provided a checklist for use by professionals, 'Is This Autism?' Although it is essentially a clinical assessment, teachers may find aspects of the checklist helpful if they are concerned about a child in their class who is displaying features of the disorder and may choose to use this checklist rather than one devised by the school or SENCO. The following headings, under which there are a number of key features to determine, are developmentally based and can provide a considerable amount of information about an individual for use in a formal diagnosis.

1. Medical history and early development which will include relevant background information.
2. General observations of the child, relating to appearance, behaviour and social development.
3. The ability of the child to attend and concentrate.
4. The child's perceptual abilities, primarily in relation to vision and hearing, as well as other senses.
5. The child's ability to use objects meaningfully, and to play constructively, socially and imaginatively.
6. The child's grasp of concepts which range from simple matching to more complex levels of understanding.
7. The child's understanding of order or sequence (both visual and auditory). The latter will include the child's interest and response to rhythm and music.
8. The child's understanding and use of speech and language.
9. The child's intellectual capability and, if old enough, his or her attainments in school.

(Source: *The Handbook of Autism* by M Aarons and T Gittens)

Teachers should feel able to make use of any information or knowledge they have about the autistic disorder to discuss their concerns with the headteacher, SENCO and the parents. Records should also be kept which will support teachers' observations and be referred to when other professionals become involved. It is at this stage that teachers may want to refer the child for further assessments. In England and Wales this will involve following the five stage model of the *Code of Practice for the Identification and Assessment of Special Educational Needs* (DfEE, 1994) whilst Northern Ireland and Scotland have a different system for formal assessment. The five stages of the Code of Practice are:

Stage 1: class or subject teachers identify or register a child's special educational needs and, consulting the school's SENCO, take initial action;

Stage 2: the school's SENCO takes a lead responsibility for gathering information and for coordinating the child's special educational provision, working with the child's teachers;

Stage 3: teachers and the SENCO are supported by specialists from outside the school;

Stage 4: the LEA considers the need for a statutory assessment and, if appropriate, makes a multi-disciplinary assessment;

Stage 5: the LEA considers the need for a Statement of special educational needs and, if appropriate, makes a Statement and arranges, monitors and reviews provision.

Implications of the Code of Practice

The Code of Practice emphasises the importance of a multi-professional approach for the identification and assessment of pupils requiring special education, which should be done in partnership with the parents. Discussions with parents have shown that they particularly welcome a diagnosis of autism or ASD because it enables them to have an explanation for their child's behaviour and also helps to determine the kind of support or education that their child will need.

The guidelines in the Code of Practice and those similarly used in other parts of the UK, regarding the assessment and Statementing of pupils identified as having special educational needs, adhere to the following principles:

- that provision matches the needs of the individual;
- that there is careful recording of the child's special educational needs, the action taken and outcomes;
- that the wishes and feelings of the child are considered;
- that there is close consultation and partnership with parents;
- that outside specialists are involved in the stage preceding referral to the LEA for a statutory assessment.

The Code of Practice does not specifically mention autism or autistic spectrum disorder but rather describes it as a learning difficulty where there is 'evidence of impaired social interaction or communication or a significantly restricted repertoire of activities, interests and imaginative development' (para. 3:57 iv). These features are also described as being found in children with emotional and behavioural difficulties (para. 3:68 iii) and speech and language difficulties (para. 3:86 iv).

The Code of Practice is currently under review and some alterations are already being considered which will have further implications for the education of children with special educational needs.

Statutory Assessments

Teachers will probably find that in discussion with the parents, they are identifying behaviours which the parents were aware of but did not consider to be much of a problem in the home situation because 'we know he has some funny habits but then we've just got used to them'.

There will be many children who have a placement in a mainstream school but are seen as having a 'non-specific' learning difficulty because their problems had not been identified as being related to ASD. The period of assessment may take several months during which time the child may have been referred to the Child and Adolescent Mental Health Services where a diagnosis of ASD or Asperger syndrome may be confirmed. The child and/or the family may also be referred to the Social Services Department for additional support such as respite and to liaise with the family regarding any post-school placement.

Some assessments, particularly IQ tests, may not be as relevant for children with ASD because they are based on abstract concepts and complex language understanding. These tests are also based on normal developmental stages but because of the patchy acquisition of skills, particularly with language, these tests may not adequately reflect how these children are functioning. The Vineland Adaptive Behaviour Scale used by educational psychologists is based on an assessment of communication, daily living skills, socialization and motor skills and may be more relevant. Some of the non-verbal aspects of the Stanford-Binet tests are also good. Similarly assessments carried out by the Speech and Language service may be able to indicate the levels of expressive and receptive language which the child is using but also need to comment on the child's 'communicative intent'.

The TEACCH programme has developed an assessment tool, the Psycho-Educational Profile (PEP), which not only identifies cognitive abnormalities but also recognises any emerging skills. Having established these it makes it possible to plan and implement an individual education plan based on what the child needs to learn as well as how they will learn.

The implications for the statutory assessments could mean that an alternative placement will need to be sought if the current provision is no longer considered appropriate. A placement can also be made where the child needs an ongoing period of assessment and the Statementing process will either be an outcome of this period of assessment or as a result of a placement in a special or mainstream school.

Parents can express a preference for their child's placement and the LEA will be expected to support parents' views. Where this involves a residential placement or a move to a different type of provision, the LEA will have a say in whether they consider this to be an appropriate use of resources.

Parents will need to determine with the LEA the most preferred placement for their child although in some parts of the country this can turn out to be the best option available rather than the most appropriate. Sadly there are children who have experienced several moves to different educational establishments supporting a particular type of teaching approach which has later been found not to be suitable for the child. It is not surprising, then, that for these children their education and personal development may become severely affected.

Issuing a Statement of Special Educational Needs (SEN)

Once all the statutory assessments have been completed at Stage 4, the LEA will decide whether to go ahead with a Statement of SEN. A Statement will be written at stage 5, although in a few cases it may be felt that a Statement will not be required. What is contained in the Statement will need to reflect the special educational needs of the individual child for whom the Statement has been written, in consultation with parents and other professionals.

In Part 2 of the Statement it should state that the child has a diagnosis of autistic spectrum disorder, autism or Asperger syndrome and, where appropriate, any additional learning difficulties. As well as stating the specific diagnosis there should also be a description of what this will mean for the child in terms of the disability. This will include how the Triad of Impairments affects the child and to what extent the child's behaviour influences his or her potential for learning.

In Part 3, there will be a description of the special educational provision based on the assessments and advice from the various agencies. It should reflect the aims and objectives for special educational provision to ensure that these meet the needs of the child and relate to the information in the previous section. In addition to the advice from parents there will need to be agreement on the opinions of all those who have submitted assessments so that the statements in this section relate to positive targets for the child to achieve. In addition, those in mainstream or in schools for children with moderate learning difficulties needing individual support by a class assistant should have the specific amount stated either in hours or days per week. It is important that the information in this section is clearly understood by the parents and all those who are working with the child since it will be used to plan the individual programme in the school. This information will also support plans for deciding upon the most appropriate placement, the details of which will be written into Part 4 of the Statement.

Details of any additional people who will be involved in the child's education will be detailed in Parts 5 and 6 of the Statement. Because of the nature of the disorder and the complexity of the language and communication difficulties, most children with an autistic spectrum disorder will require additional input from a speech and language therapist. The provision of speech and language therapy is seen as additional provision by the health authority although the LEA will have a responsibility to ensure that this provision is available. The amount of speech therapy received will, however, be dependent on the needs of the individual child with the speech and language therapist working in an advisory capacity to the teacher to ensure that programmes can be maintained in the classroom and at home.

The statutory assessments and the Statement of SEN will be completed within a set timescale and made available at the earliest date to inform parents and schools about the nature of a child's special educational needs and set out the recommendations for teaching the child.

Parents will have a right to appeal if there are discrepancies between LEA provision and the wishes of the parents for their child's education. Parents can appeal to the Special Educational Needs Tribunal if:

- the LEA refuses to make a statutory assessment of a child, after parents have asked them to;
- the LEA refuses to make a Statement for a child after an assessment;
- parents disagree with Part 2, Part 3 or Part 4 of the child's Statement, when that Statement is first made or if it is changed later;
- a child already has a Statement and the LEA refuses to assess the child again or change the name of the school in that Statement;
- the LEA decides to stop maintaining a child's Statement.

(Source: *Special Educational Needs - A Guide for Parents.* DfE, 1994)

Once a Statement of SEN has been written the school will implement an individual education plan (IEP) which relates to the targets set out in Part 3 of the Statement. The LEA will then regularly check a child's progress, usually annually, through a review of the Statement and any amendments which need to be made will be done at this time. The annual review of the Statement will be written by the class teacher who will highlight those areas of progress which the child has made over the year and identify further aims for future provision. Where these aims do not appear to reflect what is in the child's current Statement the school or LEA may request a reassessment. This could be because the current provision is no longer appropriate and a move to a mainstream or special school would be preferable or because the school feels unable to provide the resources the child needs.

CHAPTER 4
Parents as Partners

Parental Involvement

Parents have a right by law to be involved with the education of their child who has special educational needs. The Code of Practice sets out clear guidelines on how parents are to be involved and it will be the responsibility of the LEA to ensure that parents are informed of all the stages relating to educational provision whether this is in a mainstream or special school. This will mean that not only do they have a say in where they want their child to be educated but also in the planning, assessments and reviews relating to their child's education in the school. The Statementing process may be the first involvement that parents will have with the LEA and following this it will be up to the school to ensure that the wishes of the parents are being met and that liaison between parents and the teacher remain positive for the benefit of the child.

Where parents feel that a residential school is the best option for their child they will be involved in discussions with the LEA and the social services to decide whether this is the most appropriate use of resources and is in the best interests of the child for their special education provision.

Some parents who choose to have their child educated at a non-maintained or independent school at their own expense will still be involved with the LEA in the setting up and reviewing of the Statement but the LEA will not, in the majority of cases, have a responsibility for paying the school fees.

Many education authorities have now put in place a parent partnership officer who will be able to advise parents on aspects of special education and inform parents of the availability of a Named Person who can provide information and advice for parents as well as personal support. The Named Person can be a professional, a friend or relative or a member of a voluntary organisation who can be present at meetings with the LEA or go with parents when they visit the school.

In the event of parents not being happy with aspects of their child's education provision or any matter relating to the provision of a Statement, they can, having first discussed these issues with the school or education authority, appeal to the Special Needs Tribunal. The Tribunal, which is based in London, is an independent body which has no connection with any LEA. Once appeals have been heard by parents and representatives of the LEA, the Tribunal's decision will have to be upheld by all parties involved. In the majority of cases the LEA will make every effort to resolve any problems before a specific case goes to the Tribunal.

Family Issues

So far I have discussed some of the legal requirements for involving parents in their child's education but there is also the very practical daily involvement which is likely to have more influence over how well a child is doing in school. Parents often look to professionals for advice and support because they believe them to have greater knowledge and expertise about their child's disability. Parents may find, however, that this is not necessarily the case.

Families can often be confused by the diagnosis of ASD because of the different advice and opinions that they have been given by professionals explaining why their child is behaving in the ways that they do. Following a diagnosis, the process of readjustment and acceptance can be continuous especially as the parents' perceptions of their child change as they get older.

The effects of having a child with a learning difficulty in the family are far reaching, in addition to the day-to-day management of behaviour and coping with a child who has a significant social communication disorder. Many children have difficulty showing their carers affection and for some it may mean that they do not even recognise them as their parents. This can result in parents feeling that they are to blame for their child's social problems and behaviour because of the impaired relationship which they have with the child. Siblings may also feel resentment or embarrassment because their brother or sister does not react to them in the same way that others do. Consequently, they may find it difficult to have friends home if they have to explain the behaviour of their brother or sister.

Parents may feel that there is a lack of understanding by the wider population of their child's behaviour, which can frequently be misconstrued as naughty. Consequently, families can also become isolated because they are concerned about the reactions of others when they take their child out.

Schools will need to take on board some of these aspects when planning provision so that together they can support parents who are, after all, the primary carers of the child. Some parents may require counselling or support from other professionals or voluntary agencies to help with management problems and schools will need to take care not to assume that they have all the expert knowledge about a child's difficulties or future development.

Parents have a unique knowledge and understanding of their child and it will be crucial that the school does not undermine the role that parents can play in determining the priorities which they have for their child's education. Through partnership and regular meetings the school can, with the parents, decide what these priorities are going to be so that the IEP and annual review of the Statement reflect the wishes of the parents and the needs and strengths of the child.

Because the way in which these children learn can be very context bound, it can happen that they will be able to complete an independence skill in school but not at home. It will be important that teachers do not give parents the impression that they are doing something wrong at home if the child is not performing a particular skill in that situation. Likewise parents should feel able to share with teachers some of the methods they have used to encourage their child to do something if they are wanting the child to achieve it in school as well.

The nature of ASD is such that children will require an ongoing education beyond their school years and the majority of them will need to be cared for or supported in an adult residential placement or independent accommodation. Schools will need to regard themselves as part of the process of educating the child and acknowledge that there will be additional skills that such children need to learn. These may be outside the bounds of the National Curriculum but are of paramount importance to the child's future development.

Statutory and Voluntary Agencies

Where parents feel that their views are not being considered regarding their child's education they may wish to get further advice from other sources. These could include:

    a voluntary organisation
    a parent's group or
    a parent partnership adviser/officer

Throughout the country there are voluntary associations and societies which provide support for families of children and adults with ASD. The National Autistic Society (NAS) has lists of addresses and contacts, or details can be obtained from registers of voluntary agencies. These societies offer a range of services, primarily offering valuable support to families and information about education and care for children and adults with ASD. They also arrange meetings for parents and professionals where experts in the field of ASD can inform members about current medical research and education practices. Some local societies run schools for children with ASD and work in close liaison with the local education authority.

Other independent advisory services include ACE (the Advisory Centre for Education) and IPSEA (Independent Panel of Special Education Advice). A list of addresses has been included at the end of this chapter. Similar organisations operate in Wales, Scotland and Northern Ireland and addresses can be obtained from the respective government departments.

Parents should also have access to information about the support available from the Social Services who have a responsibility to provide respite for families when it is required. Children with ASD can have very complex needs but there is not always appropriate respite made available for them or their families. For many parents, there is the added problem of trying to balance the needs of their child with ASD with those of the rest of the family.

One of the outcomes of many parent support groups has been that it has given parents greater advocacy to seek better services for their children. Parent groups have been able to make representations to LEAs to request that they develop specific provision for those with autism and Asperger syndrome. Many LEAs have subsequently gone ahead with the setting up of special classes or units in mainstream and special schools as a result of parents' concerns. In some instances voluntary organisations have also set up independent schools and respite services, many of which have subsequently become centres of excellence for the care and education of these children.

Useful Addresses

Advisory Centre for Education
Unit 1B
Aberdeen Studios
22 Highbury Grove
London
N5 2DQ
Tel: 0171 354 8321 (Advice Line)

IPSEA (Main Office)
4 Ancient House Mews
Woodbridge
Suffolk
IP12 1DH
Tel: 01384 382814

National Autistic Society
393 City Road
London
EC1V 1NG
Tel: 0171 833 2299

Contact a Family
170 Tottenham Court Road
London
W1P 0HA
Tel: 0171 383 3555

Children in Scotland
Special Needs Forum
Princes House
5 Shandwick Place
Edinburgh
EH2 4RG
Tel: 0131 228 8484

The National Autistic Society in Wales
William Knox House
Suite C1 Britannic Way
Llandarcy
Neath
Port Talbot
SA10 6EL
Tel: 0179 281 5915

The National Autistic Society in Scotland
111 Union Street
Glasgow
Strathclyde
G1 3TA
Tel: 0141 221 8090

For Specialist Information:
The Centre for Social and Communication Disorders
Elliot House
113 Masons Hill
Bromley
Kent
BR2 9HT
Tel: 0181 466 0098

Early Years Diagnostic Centre
272 Longdale Lane
Ravenshead
Nottinghamshire
NG15 9AH
Tel: 01623 490879

Autism Research Unit
School of Health Sciences
University of Sunderland
Tyne and Wear
SR2 7EE
Tel: 0191 510 8922

Information for parents can also be found in: *'Special Educational Needs - a guide for parents'* published by the DfE.

Further information can also be found on the web site for the National Autistic Society
http://www.oneworld.org/autism_uk/
email: nas@mailbox.ulcc.ac.uk

CHAPTER 5
Supportive Teaching Strategies

Teaching children with special needs invariably requires a specific set of principles with which to establish educational programmes aimed at enhancing the learning outcomes for individual children. Regardless of whether a child with ASD has a placement in a specialist unit or school or is in a mainstream or special school, there are some fundamental principles which can be applied to support their learning within those environments.

The following strategies are based on a positive approach to teaching children with ASD and are certainly not the only ways that can benefit children's learning. They are based on identifying the learning strengths of the child through a structured approach to teaching. In other words, the learning environment needs to be managed in a way that gives children clearly defined activities and reduces any difficulties they may have in their response to learning. Obviously the amount of structure needed will vary between individuals and can change over time. If a child feels secure in a learning environment which provides opportunities for them to make sense of what they have to do and enables them to communicate and make choices, then there will be less need for them to resort to negative or attention-seeking behaviours. Consequently the management of behaviours which do occur can be understood in terms of the difficulties the child has because of their autism rather than any overt behaviour which is displayed.

Some of the strategies described in the following pages may be more relevant to younger children. However there are also those which will continue to be relevant to children throughout their school years. Children moving into a different environment can lose some previously acquired skills and relearning a skill in the new environment can demand that a particular strategy has to be used.

The Learning Environment

- Have areas in the classroom designated for specific activities and label what is in each of these areas with words and/or pictures.

This helps to reduce confusion and enables children to find things for themselves. It may also give them a cue as to whether they will be in that place by themselves or with a small or large group and therefore helps to prepare them for what they will be doing.

- Provide an individual work area.

This acknowledges the need for personal space and also helps them to attend to a task without other distractions. They will not always be expected to work alone but a specified area will give them an opportunity to do so when it is necessary.

- Provide access to a timetable using pictures, symbols or words.

If children know what is going to happen next using a visual cue, then they can predict what they are going to do. They may not necessarily pick up this information from what others are doing in the class, or from what they have been told. If the timetable has to be changed this also gives them time to assimilate what is happening and what the changes will mean.

- Consider sensitivity to light or to certain noises which can be very distracting and can cause distress.

Examples of this can be in the dining hall or the playground, the school bell signalling the end of lessons or even the fire bell. Children with a visual impairment may need to be seated in a certain place in the class where there is not too much light reflection or shadow.

Teaching Methods

- Present tasks using symbols or give instructions with a written list.

This helps children know what the task is, how long it is, and what is going to happen when the task is finished. They may not be able to take in too much verbal information and can therefore become confused or anxious if they do not know what they have to do.

- Do not introduce more than one skill at a time.

They may find it difficult to learn a new skill in a social situation because they are having to focus on the task in a situation which may be uncomfortable to them. If they are having to concentrate on learning to read a book, for example, they may only be able to concentrate initially on the text rather than the pictures. Describing what is happening in the picture is a different skill to reading and they may find this easier than using language to interpret the pictures. They can learn to do this once they are familiar with the text.

- Present a range of activities which will interest them and help them to develop their concentration.

If they can achieve a particular activity they will be more motivated to attend to other activities or a new task. A positive response will also encourage them to try out things for themselves.

- Be aware that they may pay attention to the trivial details of an activity and miss the point of what they are being asked to do.

Their obsessional interests may prevent them from focusing on the task they have been given. Present the task in small manageable steps so that they do not become too frustrated.

- Teach routines through a structured approach.

Children with ASD like routines which help them to understand what is expected of them. If a child has a routine for doing their number work or always choosing a certain activity first, this should be accepted or agreed with the child. Use these routines as a starting point to gradually introduce a new skill that the child needs to learn. Records will then be able to show how the child has progressed and has learnt to accept different experiences.

- Be positive and patient in your approach and be aware of how and what you are communicating to the child.

They respond better to being given clear, simple instructions rather than too many explanations of what they need to do or have not done.

Developing Relationships

- Value the child's personality and accept that they will derive their own meanings from events which may differ from what is expected.

Having poor social awareness, children may often behave in inappropriate ways and this can influence how others respond to them and reinforce their poor self-image.

25

- Acknowledge their good work with rewards and praise.

Unlike other children who will seek out approval from an adult to show their work or something they have made, those with ASD will not necessarily see the point of doing this and consequently may not share what they have done in the same way that another child would. A reward could include doing an activity of their choice.

- Encourage interaction through activities they enjoy.

Certain activities such as music lessons or preparing drinks provide opportunities for children to interact by taking turns, anticipating what is going to happen or choosing the people they want to be with. It is a feature of the developmental delay that these children will not instinctively learn to play with another child unless they are shown. Play equipment will need to be meaningful if the child is to have a positive experience through play, such as on a double swing or see-saw, or with water and sand.

- Acknowledge their need for personal space.

If children have opportunities to work independently or in a one-to-one situation this will enable them to manage more easily those times when they will need to be with others. Constantly being part of a large class or group can become stressful and result in a behaviour outburst as a way of releasing their anxiety. This is also where the visual timetable helps them to recognise when these times will occur. Some children will not like to be too close to others and therefore sitting next to the child may be more comfortable than standing over them.

- Teach them to recognise certain behaviours and emotions in others using pictures or the television.

In social situations children may become vulnerable and an 'easy target' for ridicule and bullying because they do not always understand how to respond to others. Using pictures and the television removes the 'personal' involvement and, through discussions, can help them to learn strategies for coping.

- When appropriate, teach them what a friend is.

The inability to empathise makes it difficult for them to make friends and keep them. Other children may be very tolerant of a child who they see as having some problems but they do not always find it easy to stay loyal because of other peer pressure. Children with Asperger syndrome often recognise for themselves the difficulties that they have in making friends and may try too hard to win someone's favour, perhaps inviting children to a birthday party which is several months away or offering them toys from home. Circle time, used in many schools, is an opportunity for children to share how they are feeling and also teaches them to listen to others.

- Use their own interests as a way of involving them in a social activity.

Often their isolating behaviour is a response to not knowing what to do in a social group and they can be helped to join in by sharing or showing something which interests them rather than just being passive observers.

Encouraging Communication

- For the non-verbal child, use symbols, objects of reference or pictures so that the child knows what is happening and they can also indicate what they want.

In normal development, understanding language and the use of gestures for communication occur before speech and those with a language delay will tend to use gesture or visual cues to indicate their needs to others. This is similar to the way a young baby does before they acquire speech.

There are a number of symbol systems available such as Makaton, Rebus and Pic-Sym or the teacher can create his or her own which are meaningful to an individual child. Using symbols and pictures can help to take away the awkwardness of social contact whilst enabling the child to focus on a specific task that has been given to them. A series of pictures can also be used to teach a child a skill such as dressing. By following a sequence of pictures in this way the child is also learning an important independence skill.

- Teach pointing to encourage shared attention.

Pointing, even if it is with the whole hand initially, should be encouraged so that they can make a choice of which activity they want, or which drink they would like. It is often easier to make decisions for these children thus taking away their chance to communicate and become more independent.

- Do not expect them to give eye contact.

Children's lack of eye contact reflects their inability to use it as a means of social communication and some non-verbal children will use eye contact only to gain attention. It is important not to make the child feel uncomfortable if they are not able to offer eye contact as it may be that just standing or sitting close to someone is a sufficient achievement for him or her at that time.

- Verbal instructions should be brief and simple.

Even children with language may have difficulties listening to instructions, not because they have problems with comprehension but with the communication of ideas from another person. Also, being able to communicate in a positive way, eg 'we are going outside' rather than 'shall we go?' will help to set an expectation for a certain behaviour and reduce the uncertainty of what might happen.

- Always begin an instruction using the child's name to gain their attention.

This will help to gain their attention and enable them to recognise an instruction directed to them, otherwise they may miss the point of what they have been asked to do.

- Recognise that their receptive and expressive language skills do not follow the normal developmental patterns.

There is a tendency to assume that the non-verbal child will acquire fewer skills because they do not have the linguistic understanding. In most cases it is a problem with social communication not language, since the receptive skills tend to be much better than the expressive ones. For those with good language skills the situation is often reversed in that there can be an overestimation of their abilities as they are likely to have difficulties developing abstract concepts and ideas in conversations.

- Encourage imitation and co-operation.

Children will often echo what has been said to them or repeat familiar phrases. By teaching specific phrases in context it will help the child to learn the language required for that situation. This may appear not to be a spontaneous use of language but it will help them to use the appropriate language in context and they are more likely to co-operate if what they say has been acknowledged.

- Recognise that they will interpret information in very literal ways and may have difficulty understanding innuendo and jokes.

It is a feature of the way in which they interpret information that these children will be very literal in what they say and what is said to them. Often this can give rise to awkward situations and can cause distress to the child if their subsequent responses are misunderstood. One young boy who was told to 'wipe his feet' as he came in from the playground, took off his shoes and socks and wiped his feet. He had literally done as he was told! Teachers can often inadvertently use phrases or sayings which other children can see the point of but could be beyond the comprehension of the child with ASD, eg 'Go and bury your head in a book for ten minutes.'

- Teach children to interpret body language and facial expressions.

Communication is not just about using words but involves a whole complex system of signs and hidden agendas. Because they will not learn through their own or others' body language they will need to be taught, using pictures, the computer or the television, a range of different emotions and facial expressions. It is also important that adults are aware of what and how they are communicating to the child, their tone of voice, facial expressions and their body language.

- Recognise the difficulty they have using 'I' and 'You'.

Because their ability to see themselves in relation to others is impaired, they will tend to use their own or the person's name rather than the personal pronoun. It can be regarded as rudeness or laziness but is in fact a feature of the developmental delay in language. It may help when talking to them to tell them what is happening, rather than just doing it so that they learn to recognise the difference between what they are doing in relation to someone else, eg 'I am going to sit down, you are going to the playground', and accompany this with a visual cue by pointing to them.

- Teach language and naming objects in context and through functional activities.

Language is best learnt in the context in which it occurs so that it is meaningful and provides opportunities for repetition and consolidation. Functional activities should be planned to encourage naming objects or actions, eg making meals, shopping, dressing, or caring for their personal hygiene.

- Teach them to ask questions and not just follow rules.

In the early years of normal language development, one and two word utterances are used to ask questions and make requests. If these are used in context as an indication of something the child wants then it will be important that they get a positive response. Repetitive questioning can be an indication of stress and a means of gaining attention but nonetheless it is important that some response is given otherwise they will not see the point of using language to express their needs.

- Respond to any attempts to use language.

Even if the child uses an inappropriate phrase or vocalises in response to something they are doing, these should be responded to in the context of where they occurred. Some children often respond better when sung to rather than when spoken to because the modulation of the voice alters and can be more interesting to them. If they then imitate what they have heard they may continue a two-way conversation by singing and involving themselves in interaction.

- Teach them what communication is.

Non-verbal children tend to use physical gestures to indicate their needs, eg taking an adult's hand to what they want. This is important as it is a means of interaction which they have chosen. If on the other hand they resort to aggressive behaviour as a demand for something they want, this needs to be replaced by teaching them to use symbols or pictures so that the interaction is positive.

Turn taking activities can happen in a variety of different situations, eg with music, during register time or playing with a favourite toy. More able children will need to be taught how to take turns in a conversation, how close they stand when they are talking to someone and that the topic of conversation should be interesting for both people. Again, Circle Time can help to teach these skills.

Managing Behaviour

- Disapprove of the behaviour, not the child.

It is often the case that we put greater expectations on socially appropriate behaviour from those with a disability than we do from those who do not. For this reason there will be some behaviours which occur as a result of the difficulties they have because of the autism and behaviours which happen because they are children living in families which have their own set of rules and expectations. It will therefore be important to recognise that there is a difference between what is 'naughty' behaviour, and therefore normal, and what is 'autistic' behaviour, and that they behave in different ways because they are children, who also have a disability.

- Provide clear and explicit boundaries for behaviour.

Children should realise that they cannot have everything their own way. If it is a rule to sit quietly for a certain activity then talking should not be allowed by any member of the class. Making allowances for the one child can invite them to behave differently in other situations.

- Give tangible rewards and praise.

Rewards can be given which help the child to recognise that something they have done has pleased the adult working with them. A reward will need to be something which is meaningful to the child and relates to the activity they have just completed, eg when a child finishes a set task then they can choose an activity they like. Such rewards can be very motivating as the child will be more prepared to complete a task knowing that there is something they enjoy, following it. In the same way that if a child eats something they have not tried before then he can eat his favourite food as a reward. The use of food rewards for doing good work will not necessarily help the child to understand why he has done that particular activity.

- Recognise situations which might cause distress or a behaviour problem.

Children are very individual in the way that they respond to different situations which is why it is very important to identify these in their assessments. The demands of a social group or over-stimulation can affect their ability to concentrate and behaviour can deteriorate. Removing the child or the stimulus can be a way of avoiding a difficult situation and an alternative activity can be made available. In the same way aggressive behaviour should not be seen as a direct attack on a person but a reaction to a frightening or frustrating situation which the child cannot express in ways that others might.

Gary LaVigna, a child psychiatrist, once stated that 'All behaviour has message value.' This does not mean that all behaviours are intrinsically good but that they serve to explain or communicate an emotion or some physical state.

- Sanctions and punishments need to be immediate and meaningful otherwise they will not be understood in relation to what the child has done.

These children experience the world very much in the present and will not necessarily see the point of sanctions or understand the effect that their behaviour has on others. In the same way 'time out' is least effective if it is a chance to be away from an activity that they did not want to be involved in. Isolating the child who is already having difficulties with the social demands of learning does not actually help the child learn how they could behave in a group situation. Altering or redirecting an activity in these circumstances is more effective and also means that they are still working within the boundaries set by the teacher rather than having to resort to other punitive measures.

- Tell the child what to do rather than not what to do.

As these children are likely to have a problem comprehending the feelings of others they will not necessarily understand the consequences of their behaviour. A child who is repeatedly doing something they have been told not to is in fact gaining positive feedback from the attention the behaviour is getting. If for example a child is banging the table the appropriate response would be 'keep your hands still' rather than, 'stop banging the table'. The child may only hear 'bang... table' and therefore continue to do it. Using 'no' can often be the stimulus to continue the behaviour.

- Acknowledge behaviours which indicate stress.

Hand flapping, inappropriate giggling, squealing or repetitive questioning are all behaviours which may indicate that they are concerned about the situation they are in. Interpreting these in this way may mean that a child can be removed briefly from the situation therefore avoiding a tantrum and potential problems for other children in the class. The ritualistic behaviours can also serve as a comfort and a way of imposing sameness in their environment. Not all these rituals, however, are necessarily interfering with their learning. If a child is not comfortable sitting to do an activity unless they remove their shoes then it would be better for the shoes to be left off so that they can achieve the task. In this way the learning experience is a positive one rather than one which can ultimately leave the child distressed.

- Be aware of sensitivity to advice and criticism.

More able children may feel that they are always being told what to do and can give the impression they can do things when in fact they are uncertain of what is required. Rather than point this out to them, ask them for their suggestions on how they would do it and invite them to join in. Practical activities are often a better way of involving them than social ones. For example, a child wanted to make a cake and told the teacher he knew what to do. When he had not begun the activity the teacher prompted him by saying, 'You get the flour out of the cupboard and I'll find the margarine.' This helped the child to begin the task and also removed the likelihood of him feeling a failure. They may need constant reassurance that they are behaving properly in a certain situation. One child was frequently asking 'Am I being good?' as his way of determining what he was doing.

- Set limits on obsessive and ritualistic behaviours.

Children who have difficulty interpreting the world around them will seek out objects which interest them and unlike people, these are predictable and therefore make them safe to be with. An environment which is structured to provide a variety of different experiences will mean that they can learn new skills and the time spent in an isolated state with their obsessional interests will be lessened. Leaving a child 'twiddling' because it is assumed that it makes them happy is in fact denying them access to opportunities to learn and interact with people. A child's obsessional interest can become the focus for topic work and be developed by exploring various aspects of it through the curriculum subjects.

- Be consistent in your responses to behaviour.

Children will need to learn which behaviours are acceptable and which ones are not. The IEP should provide information about how a particular behaviour is being managed and where appropriate this can be negotiated with the child so that they can learn to have some responsibility for their actions. If children are not managed consistently by those around them then they can become confused and may not then learn about the social expectations of their behaviour. These children do not always plan to behave negatively, nor do they seek to gain pleasure from the consequences of their behaviour. This is because there are explanations for some of their behaviour such as pain, confusion and frustration which once again should not be interpreted in the same way as misbehaviour. They may recognise that a certain behaviour gets a reaction or some attention by an adult but it is more likely to be a response to a certain pattern of behaviour rather than an intention to interact.

Summary

A placement which can be described as 'appropriate' for an individual child is one where their disability is acknowledged and understood in terms of how they are being taught and this can occur in a variety of different educational settings. The teaching methods will need to address the Triad of Impairments at all levels of ability. This is because the way in which these children interpret and use information, their difficulties with communication and social interaction and their patterns of behaviour significantly affect their response to learning.

Schools will have to consider how much the learning environment facilitates the development of *communication, motivation, organisation* and *independence* through a variety of different experiences and functional activities, within the National Curriculum. In the different classroom settings, staff can then plan a way of delivering the curriculum which acknowledges:

- how and what the child communicates;
- what motivates the child;
- how to structure activities to encourage learning; and
- what opportunities there are for developing independence.

CHAPTER 6
Accessing the National Curriculum

All children regardless of their disability have a right of access to the National Curriculum. For most children with ASD this will also mean that in addition to the National Curriculum subjects there will need to be an emphasis on teaching communication and social skills. This implies that they will benefit from a much broader curriculum to ensure that the skills they will need for adulthood can be established as early as possible in their school career.

The programmes of study outlined in the National Curriculum imply that children will learn and develop their knowledge through interaction with their peers which for some children with ASD will be very difficult. Some subjects may be readily accessible to such children because of their content or style of delivery, whereas those which require an understanding of language and fiction, such as History and English, or focus on group work, such as Drama and PE, may require some adaptations to be made.

Because of the patchy acquisition of skills it may not always be possible to recognise progression through the key stages. Consequently testing could indicate failure whereas the level of achievement for an individual child could be particularly relevant given the additional time they have needed to practise the skills they have learnt.

Children in schools for severe learning difficulties (SLD) are likely to have significantly fewer language skills and more disruptive behaviours which may affect their ability to access some areas of the National Curriculum. For these children the curriculum will probably include a greater focus on the development of communication and the teaching of personal and independence skills since for them, there is as much value in achieving skills in these areas as there is for others who will gain some academic qualification.

The following paragraphs will look at the different subject areas and suggest some ways in which adaptations can be made or where additional support might be required. It will also identify some areas where children with ASD might excel and therefore benefit from some additional input in those subjects.

ENGLISH
Speaking and Listening
This is an area which can be difficult for many children with ASD. If a child is having difficulties attending to instructions or a conversation it may help if they are directed to them, rather than the whole class and said in the context of what is happening. It may be that the child could be given a written script of the main points of what is being discussed which they can have time to study and respond to in an appropriate way at a later stage.

Children who are mute will need to have an alternative means of communication, either with symbols, objects of reference or written words so that they can make their needs known or indicate through pictures what is happening in a particular situation. Again, if an activity is meaningful to the child it will gain their attention and they will be more likely to attend to what they are being asked to do. For those with emerging speech, teaching them a set phrase or sentence for a particular activity will mean that they can learn to use an appropriate response. As previously mentioned, their use of language can be very context bound and things they may say at home may not occur in school. This is why it is important to share information with parents and record what the child can do, without limiting it just to the classroom situation. A child who in class used very limited phrases to express what he wanted, at home would occasionally tell his mother what he was doing using whole sentences and would briefly maintain a conversation.

More able children will also need to be taught about the timing of conversations, eye contact and social proximity so that their difficulties in this area are not so noticeable. If they recognise through others' responses that they are not doing it correctly there may be significant changes in their behaviour which could emphasize the difficulties they are having.

There will be some children who will want to talk continually about their interests and obsessions and they will need to be taught to recognise when this is allowed and that the person they are talking to might not be as interested in the subject as they are. To enable them to contribute in the class, their particular interest could be brought into the topic which will give them an opportunity to share it with the class, but remember to tell them how long they can have to talk about it!

Reading

Children need to learn that a set of symbols, including words, have meaning and carry information. Because the perceptual skills of those with ASD are often well developed, they can learn to read using symbols or words quite early on in their development. It should not be assumed that because a child is not using language to communicate then they are unable to read. This is an example of where their skills do not follow the normal patterns of development recognised in other children and it will be important not to undermine their reading potential because they are not able to use speech. There have been children for whom understanding or recognising words and symbols has encouraged the development of speech, which is contrary to the normal routes one would expect.

They are more likely to recognise a word by its shape which if it is used continually in the same context will be learnt quite quickly. The 'look and say' approach to reading can therefore be more effective than the phonetic approach which requires the children to have an understanding of how sound patterns fit together and is a much more complex skill (although for some children this can become a fascination).

Teachers will need to be aware that some children will look at books not because of their content but because they like the sensation of moving the pages. Encouraging them to gain meaning from a book, can be done by making up a book using photographs of people, objects or places which are familiar to the child and labelling it so that the child has an opportunity to learn from it. Using words as well as pictures also provides an opportunity to progress to recognising the words in different contexts. Recognising 'cake' with the symbol or picture, learning the word 'cake' and then recognising it on packets in the supermarket, is an example of such a learning progression.

Some children may read very well but have little understanding of what they are reading. This is termed 'hyperlexia' and can give the impression that because the child is reading well then they have good verbal comprehension, whereas in fact they do not. Teaching the child to read words or recognise symbols by labelling everyday objects or reading about topics which interest them will also help to develop skills in comprehension.

Writing

Many children will have difficulties with motor coordination and may not be able to form letters well. It will be important not to be too critical of their efforts but to provide many opportunities for practice. If the child has particularly good computer skills they may feel more confident using this instead of becoming anxious about writing. The concept keyboard can be prepared similarly to the QWERTY keyboard if the child has difficulties identifying the letters on the conventional keyboard.

Using rhymes to help them form letters can be particularly beneficial as they might enjoy the repetition of the rhyme when they are writing. They may also appreciate a lot of opportunities to practise because once they have mastered the skills required they are likely to develop a fascination for writing especially if they are able to write about their favourite topic.

One major area of difficulty for these children could be in writing stories which require them to use their imagination. They will need considerable help in this area which may mean providing them with cue cards, getting them started with a sentence or providing them with a list of ideas in the order that they want to put them in the story. Some children appear to develop an imaginative sense but it is likely that they have used stories they already know or have watched on the television. If the teacher recognises this, through discussion with the child, they can help them to bring in other ideas around a basic story outline.

In this example written by a child aged 12 with Asperger syndrome, there is evidence that she has an understanding of story structure. Using a familiar story animal she has been able to include aspects of her own experience and has interpreted the imaginative ideas through factual information which is very significant to her.

THE LOST DRAGON

Once there was a Dragon who was lonely. He had no friends and no family.

Roberta, a kind and lovely girl found the Dragon in a cave. The Dragon was rather happy cos Roberta had said she liked Dragons. "I have Asperger syndrome", said Roberta, sadly "so I can't understand some things".

"Well", said the Dragon kindly, "Get on my back."
"Why?", asked Roberta.

"Because I know everything", said the Dragon. So Roberta got on his back.
"I will show you everything from up here", said the Dragon and flew up into the sky. "Up here", said the Dragon.

Roberta asked the Dragon, "can humans fly?". "No", said the Dragon, "I have wings. When I flap them it puffs up the air, but gravity would pull you down".

Roberta was curious, she thought, "I will jump off the Dragon's back and see what happens". So Roberta stood up and before the Dragon could tell her not to, Roberta jumped off his back, spreading her arms out, flapping, trying to fly.

The Dragon was very angry, he swooped down and grabbed Roberta with his huge claws. He held her tight so he wouldn't drop her and looked around for somewhere safe to land. The Dragon saw some moorland ahead, it was beautiful and full of wild flowers and had a lake. The Dragon couldn't land with Roberta in his claws, so he dropped her in the lake!

"Help", shouted Roberta, "I can't swim". The Dragon landed quickly and cupped his large claws and scooped her out of the water. "I am angry", said the Dragon.

"Why?", said Roberta.
"I told you humans couldn't fly and you wouldn't listen. This is part of your Asperger syndrome", said the Dragon. "We will build a fire so you can dry your clothes and while you are drying I will explain about things you must not do".

Roberta collected some sticks and built a bonfire, the Dragon blew fire out of his mouth on to the sticks and logs. The Dragon put one of his claws on the ground and Roberta sat on it, he lay the other one over her legs to keep her warm.

"Now Roberta", said the Dragon very seriously. "You must never jump from my back, it's very dangerous. If you had hit the ground, you would have been killed".

34

"What's killed mean?", asked Roberta.

"Killed means you die".

"What does die mean?", asked Roberta.

"Die means the end of your life", said the Dragon.

"Now I know, said Roberta, "I had a baby sister called Becky, she died, so I know its the end of your life".

"Why did your sister die?", asked the Dragon.

"I don't know", said Roberta.

"What did your mother say about your sister's illness?".

"She said it was Whooping Cough"

"Oh dear that is sad", said the Dragon. "Are you afraid of anything?"

"What do you mean?, I don't understand afraid", Roberta said.

The Dragon explained that to understand that some things are dangerous you must feel what it is to be afraid.

The warm fire makes them both sleepy. The Dragon falls asleep and Roberta plans her next adventure.

MATHEMATICS

For many children the rote learning of numbers and different formulae will be easier to master than other elements of the mathematics curriculum which are based on the child's abilities in verbal reasoning and learning mathematical concepts based on comprehension. There may be difficulties in sequencing skills and the ability to predict and these will need to be taught through practical examples with a lot of over-learning.

Wherever possible use practical examples to help the child consolidate their understanding or use objects which interest them as a starting point for teaching a particular concept. If a child has a fascination for green bricks, use these to build a tower with other green bricks to teach them to count, or introduce red bricks with green bricks to encourage matching. Concepts such as big and little, more and less, same and different, can also be taught using familiar objects so that they can develop a visual understanding of the problem without being so dependent on the need to use and interpret language.

Shopping and cooking will engage them in the practical application of using money and weights rather than trying to learn these concepts only through problem solving exercises.

Again, where a child is not able to write down solutions to a problem, they should have the opportunity to record it in a way that is meaningful to them which could be using objects or symbols or a computer printout to represent their answers.

SCIENCE

For most children, exploring and investigating their environment is something that they enjoy doing and activities will be meaningful to them if they are given opportunities to take part in everyday tasks. It will therefore be relevant, through the curriculum activities, to provide some direction to these activities otherwise they may still not understand the purpose of a particular task such as personal care, or recognise the dangers of touching certain substances which are likely to cause them harm.

More able children will be able to write and even talk about the factual information but may have difficulties with group activities and explaining the 'how' and 'why' questions which they need to do to extend their understanding. They are likely to need some additional class support so that they can consolidate their understanding of a particular activity and to ensure that they do handle different substances safely.

Many children will have a fascination for touching, smelling and feeling and for those with more severe learning difficulties access to a sensory approach to the curriculum will provide opportunities for extending their interests through topic work. An obsessional interest in water is quite common amongst children with ASD but through topic work their fascination can be directed to learning about the different properties and uses of water with as much practical work as possible, eg making hot and cold drinks, watering plants, washing up or washing clothes.

Opportunities for environmental work should be included as much as possible so that the children have an opportunity to see things in the right context and can record details with photographs or writing so that they can reflect on the experience. Even electricity pylons and air vents have been a great source of photographic interest to some children who could then use these to learn about power and energy.

Teaching children about human development and reproduction is another area of the curriculum where they may have difficulties making connections between themselves and the factual information they are learning. It is also closely linked to how these children see themselves in relation to others so it will be important to extend this area of learning into their social skills training as there are significant implications for teaching appropriate behaviour especially with regards to sex education.

DESIGN AND TECHNOLOGY

In a similar way to science activities, children will enjoy the practical manipulation of a range of materials but they may require direction if they are to achieve making something. They are often more interested in taking things apart than they are in putting them back together again!

Because of their difficulties with imagination and sequencing they may find it hard to plan and follow a design. A good starting point will be to have a model of what they are expected to produce and a list of stages, either written or in pictures which are simple enough for them to understand. If they have a problem with motor coordination they may need some adapted tools to help them and these should be identified before the child is put into a situation where they are not managing. Topics will also need to be planned to take account of their interests, for example they may be interested in making rockets and cars but not so keen on designing a game. If the child has difficulties explaining how they made something then they should be able to present this work either by writing it down or drawing pictures to show what they did.

INFORMATION COMMUNICATION TECHNOLOGY

For many children using a computer is a skill which is superior to any others they have and they can be remarkably adept at using the different components. For some it develops into an obsessional interest but this is understandable when they feel more comfortable interacting with a computer than with a person.

For children with more severe learning difficulties, it can be used to encourage them to point, using a touch screen, so that they learn about cause and effect and have opportunities to develop their hand/eye coordination. Programs will need to be carefully chosen and a time limit set, to ensure that the child is developing skills they need and that the computer is not just available to keep them occupied.

Computer assisted learning is particularly relevant for these children and should be used wherever possible to support their access to other subjects. Where children have difficulties with writing or expressing themselves verbally they should have access to a computer to help them present work that is required. There are a range of interactive programs which require the child to ask an adult for assistance to move on to the next stage, and of course using the computer is highly motivating. Often the computer can be used as a means for developing language and numeracy skills, particularly if the teacher or assistant working with the child recognises how the skills they have learnt on the computer can be used in other contexts.

HISTORY

Although these children have very good long-term memory skills and can remember places and people with a remarkable ability, they may have little understanding of past cultures and times in history since these involve understanding people's behaviour and events which have affected people's lives. They tend to live very much in the present, and therefore may have poor understanding of the effect of events that have happened in the past or of what is going to happen in the future.

A child may be able to learn by rote a list of dates and events in the past since these are concrete, factual pieces of information but they might have difficulties trying to describe 'A Day in the Life of a Roman', which would require them to use their imaginative and linguistic skills.

Photographs of past events they have been involved in or pictures of themselves as a baby may help them to get a sense of 'the past', or the death of an elderly relative may start them asking questions but it is likely that historical events will only be understood if they relate to their experiences. Pictures or films on the television could be used as a starting point for discussions which could then be supported with a list of written cues to help them if they are going to do a written exercise.

GEOGRAPHY

Many parents will recall how their child has a remarkable memory for remembering the routes that are taken to get to school or to the shops and how any deviation from the route can cause a reaction. Some children are fascinated by road signs, road numbers and even the numbers on the telegraph poles, all of which suggest that they have a natural awareness of their surroundings. These examples come from their need to order their world in terms of the visual information which they can interpret. Map reading may therefore be a strength for some children with ASD since they appear to enjoy representing features in lines and can incorporate their mathematical understanding of scale as well.

Learning about their immediate environment will be important. For some it may mean learning to move independently within their familiar environment or having experiences of the local shopping area and using buses or trains.

Many children are fascinated by geological structures and the physical elements of geography. I know of children whose topic of interest has involved detailed studies and record keeping of the global effects of earthquakes, volcanoes and tidal waves.

Other children as they get older develop a sense of themselves in their culture and through their social experiences but those with ASD will not necessarily be able to understand this in the same way and may be confused by events and discussions which take place. Using pictures or artifacts and opportunities to explore different environments can help to consolidate their understanding.

Their understanding of different cultures and different ways of life can be learnt through listening to the music of that country and wearing clothes or eating food from that country, all of which can provide a valuable experience for them and are possibly more meaningful than copying information from texts. If the child goes on holiday they could bring in photographs to show what it is like and possibly even recall details of the places they visited. In this way they could be learning about a different place within the context of what they are learning in the lesson.

PHYSICAL EDUCATION

Many children with ASD show a remarkable agility with running and climbing whilst others may be ill coordinated and find many physical activities difficult to master. This can also be related to their difficulties with imitating the actions of others and understanding the social rules in games. Consequently they may prefer to opt out of lessons rather than put themselves in a situation which they cannot cope with.

Overcoming some of these problems can be done by planning a lesson where they are working in a small group and only need to focus on one piece of apparatus. Where possible it may also be important to choose a group of children to work with who will encourage rather than make fun of the efforts the child is making.

Where some children may be happy to present their work to others, the child with ASD may feel uncomfortable doing this and a few words of encouragement to the child may be preferred rather than having to show their good work in front of the class.

If a child has problems taking part in team games it may be that they could have a responsibility for keeping the score. Often learning the rules of the game can be easier for them rather than taking part, especially if they do so with the ridicule or annoyance of other members of the team.

It is worth noting that many children with ASD will gain a lot of pleasure from the dance element of the curriculum. Dance can be particularly therapeutic and can be an opportunity for self-expression, and very different from the need to conform in other physical exercises. It is also quite likely that given this opportunity, they will be happy to work in a small group, bringing their ideas for a topic or theme from something they have been learning about in another area of the curriculum. In one science class the children had been learning about heat and during a dance session coloured scarves were used and the children created a small dance piece moving with the scarves around each other like flames.

ART

There are several cases where children with ASD have been found to have a special skill in drawing, particularly buildings and still life. These children clearly have a highly developed visual perception which enables them to recall with amazing detail, what they have seen. However, such skills are not present in the majority of people with ASD and many will be functioning very much at a sensory level in terms of their exploration of textures and different media. Some children have a phobia about getting any substances on their hands and will not be willing to investigate different materials whereas others may have a fascination for certain colours or even tasting paint and glue!

Experiences should be offered which enable children to explore and use a range of different materials to develop an understanding of the range of effects that can be achieved. It may not be so easy for them to talk about their work or describe what they are doing as they are required to do in the programmes of study. They may find it easier to cope with the creative elements of the course work and have difficulty developing a knowledge and understanding of art or being able to comment on the work of other artists. Keeping a sketch book or portfolio of their work could help them to reflect on what they have done and they could be encouraged to collect pictures or photographs of artists' work which support their own work.

Art also has therapeutic benefits for these children and can be used to encourage them to interact at a very personal level, by exploring colours, shapes and textures. Art therapy is a very specialised approach and can be used with children who have severe learning difficulties or who are experiencing psychological or emotional problems.

MUSIC

The creative, expressive and social aspects of music teaching can never be underestimated when working with these children. Music works as a tool for developing communication at several different levels and therefore has a valuable role to play in the education of children with ASD. Children may respond well to the repetition of a rhythm and to familiar tunes which can be used to encourage speech. Skills such as turn taking, anticipating and attention can be taught through songs and using instruments.

Children with no speech can choose which song they would like to sing by selecting a toy or object which represents a song. One child who loved singing but did not want to sit in a group, was encouraged to join in by choosing a toy which represented a song. Once he had done this he would sit down with the group and begin the singing. Objects or instruments can also be passed around to encourage children to share and take turns so that at the same time, they are learning an important social skill and developing an awareness of others in the group.

Some children appear to gain a lot of pleasure from repetitive banging or exploring the sounds of percussion instruments. Whilst this can be used in a therapeutic way to encourage a 'conversation' or turn taking activity children also need to be taught how to listen to a rhythm and the beat of a tune so that they can learn to accompany it. If a child is able to follow a simple tune, the notes on the instrument can be colour coded or numbered so that they can follow a 'musical score' which does not have to be written in musical notation.

There will be a few children who will have an exceptional talent for music, can sing in tune often with perfect pitch and can play a piece of music after hearing it only once. Skills such as this should be encouraged so that the child has an opportunity to develop his or her skills. However, this will not always mean that they will want to perform for others. This could be a skill which interests them but they may not necessarily see it as something to share with other people.

Music as therapy has been used very successfully with children with ASD, in encouraging children to use their voices and eventually to develop speech. It has also been effective in encouraging the very withdrawn child to interact through using instruments. Many of the techniques used in music therapy can be adapted for the classroom but music therapy on a one-to-one or group basis should be run by someone with a recognised qualification.

RELIGIOUS EDUCATION

All children are required by law to have some religious education within the curriculum. Children can be taught the relevance of religion to different cultures and the religious practices which go with them through a sensory approach, making use of candles, smells, music or visits to churches and temples or inviting people of different cultures and religions into the school. Religious festivals can also be experienced in the same way at the appropriate times of the year and include all the foods, clothes and colours which relate to them.

Most schools adhere to an act of worship and children will learn songs and listen to stories from Christian teaching and from other religions. Children with ASD may not necessarily recognise these times as different from other activities they do during the day and for some, sitting in a hall or classroom with a lot of other children can be a distressing or confusing experience.

More able children who learn or read stories from the bible may possibly only interpret it on the basis of factual evidence rather than whether it has any religious meaning. Similarly they may not be able to relate certain social behaviours to a religious or moral standpoint but can be taught about good or inappropriate behaviour through their daily activities and personal and social education.

PERSONAL, SOCIAL AND HEALTH EDUCATION (PSHE)

Although this is not a separate subject within the National Curriculum it is, however, seen as an important element of teaching since it is relevant across all the subject areas.

In this chapter there has been a lot of emphasis on the need to teach children with ASD through a variety of practical and everyday experiences. Social skills training will be a vital aspect of all teaching and time should be set aside for children with good language skills to talk about relevant subjects in groups, such as Circle Time. This could include what it feels like to have autism, encouraging the child to say what they find difficult so that other children and the teacher or assistant can gain an insight into how they are thinking and feeling. Much like a child with a physical disability has to overcome problems of mobility so a child with ASD will need help to learn how to manage in social situations that they find difficult.

Children will have to be taught how to behave towards those of both sexes as they get older and to recognise dangers and vulnerable situations. They may need to learn how to share or take turns in a conversation so that others do not get cross with them, sometimes learning what to say so that they do not embarrass themselves or others.

There will be some children who experience bullying in the playground because they can be an easy target for ridicule and do not necessarily understand how to defend themselves or walk away from awkward situations. Staff will need to be aware of children for whom this may be a constant problem and alternative arrangements made so that they do not have to go outside but can remain inside with a chosen companion.

Many children with severe learning difficulties will have significant problems with personal care, toileting, washing and dressing. They may have phobias about eating certain foods or their sleeping patterns may be very erratic and these can significantly affect their behaviour. Where a child is having particular difficulties, these will need to be identified in their IEP and worked on consistently so that the child can develop greater independence in their personal care.

Not all problem behaviours will disappear but with a programme of intervention they can be limited or reduced. This will enable them to learn from other experiences rather than being so dependent on specific patterns of behaviour or their obsessions.

Teaching personal and independence skills can sometimes seem like a continual struggle and it is easy to see why some parents and teachers decide that they are no longer going to focus on teaching a particular skill. This is because for many children, their inability to learn a new skill is part of a ritualistic pattern of behaviour which they cannot easily change. Also some children will eventually acquire skills because they have reached a level of maturity where they can do something spontaneously without it needing to be taught.

The very passive child may not initiate dressing themselves and expect an adult to do it for them. Often the child can have very good fine motor skills when handling things that they have an obsessional interest in, but cannot manage to put on their clothes or do up buttons, zips or shoes. Many children are reluctant to use their hands for independent tasks and every opportunity should be used to encourage the child to do things for themselves. The child could be involved with the adult's hand over the child's so that they gain an awareness of what they are doing rather than what is happening to them or for them.

Some more able children may have developed specific rituals for dressing and washing and it will be helpful to teachers if parents can let them know if their child does, otherwise problems can occur during school or when changing for PE or swimming if the teacher or support assistant is not aware of this.

Wherever possible more able children should learn how to use the shops and local transport and develop basic skills in cooking, making drinks and budgeting as these are all skills they will need for adulthood.

All children will have personalities and skills which are unique to them and it will be important to make those with ASD feel they are liked because of them. By teaching relevant skills and offering a range of experiences this will help children with ASD to develop their sense of self-worth and enable them to recognise that they are valued members of their class, school and community.

CHAPTER 7
Writing Individual Education Plans

The individual education plan will be the important document describing the pupil's short-term needs and the special teaching arrangements which will be required to meet them. At Stages 2-5 of the Code of Practice an IEP will be implemented and will subsequently be maintained by the school SENCO or headteacher, with the class teacher. Whether a child is attending a mainstream or special school, the statutory advice will be similar and schools will have the option to use a planned format for the IEP or to devise their own. Whichever one is adopted it will need to include the following elements:

- the nature of the pupil's difficulties;
- action - the special educational provision;
    - staff involved including frequency of support;
    - specific programmes, activities, materials, equipment;
- help from parents at home;
- targets to be achieved in a given time;
- any pastoral care or medical requirements;
- monitoring and assessment arrangements;
- other support agencies involved;
- review arrangements and date.

Nature of Pupil's Difficulties

The information acquired from the various assessments and teacher observations should give an indication of the child's difficulties and level of functioning. For children with ASD, there will need to be an explanation of what this will mean in terms of their communication skills, their cognitive abilities and their behaviour which will affect their response to the learning environment. Any additional difficulties which the child may have, such as epilepsy or a physical disability, will also affect their learning and have implications for other resources they may need.

Teachers will need to recognise individual differences and abilities so that the learning is relevant for the child. This can be based on an assessment using the following criteria:

PERSONAL FACTORS
- the child's strengths and weaknesses
- developmental level and any emerging skills
- communication skills
- independence skills
- personality

SOCIAL FACTORS
- how the child relates to peers and adults
- do they prefer to be alone?
- how they manage in a group
- response to the learning environment
- are they easily distracted?

BEHAVIOUR
- what types of behaviour are displayed?
- any aggressive or self-injurious behaviours

- when and where the behaviours occur
- nature of obsessional interests
- what is their reaction to intervention?

Action - Special Education Provision

Whether a child has a placement in a mainstream or special school or unit there will need to be close collaboration within the school to ensure that the methods of working with children with ASD in the classroom are supported through a whole school policy.

The Code of Practice states that the plan, 'should usually be implemented, at least in part, in the normal classroom setting,' and that 'the plan should build on the curriculum the child is following alongside fellow pupils'. For those with ASD this might involve the child spending time either in a learning support unit or in a special class for some areas of the curriculum. The special education provision will be one which emphasises an individual approach to teaching whether they are taught in a specialist class or in a class with children who may or may not have learning difficulties.

Children in special schools may be receiving their education in classes where there are likely to be children with a range of other learning disabilities. Where specialist provision has been set up within these environments children will have access to an environment which supports their learning needs while providing opportunities within the school for them to take part in activities with their peers to enhance their social and personal development.

Children in the mainstream schools who are part of a larger class group are likely to need the support of a learning support assistant (LSA) who should have knowledge of the autistic disorder so that they understand some of the difficulties a child is having and can recognise the triggers for certain behaviours. Careful consideration will need to be given to the amount of support given and when it is given so that the child does not feel singled out by having an adult with them or that they spend so much time with the support assistant that there is little opportunity for them to work with others in the class.

In supporting the child in the mainstream classroom, teachers will need to take account of:

- the provision of ancillary or teaching support and the hours per week specified;
- the provision of a withdrawal facility for curriculum support or social skills training;
- the provision of speech and language therapy or other agency involvement and the number of hours specified;
- the provision of additional materials and resources, eg pictorial or written timetables, cue cards to support different subject areas, adapted equipment.

Targets

The targets in the IEP should be realistic, relevant and reachable. This could be regarded as a new definition of the 3Rs which permeate through all aspects of the curriculum. Schools will have chosen a system whereby they can highlight a set of short-term and long-term aims, eg termly and yearly.

In devising achievable targets, the assessments and observations will be an important starting point for planning a pupil's learning outcomes. Targets will include the educational aims as well as any personal, social skills and behaviours which need to be focused on. Where the National Curriculum subjects have been identified, these should show how they are to be differentiated to suit the needs of a particular child, if it is appropriate. Targets should focus on emerging skills so that they can be recorded at a later date as positive outcomes. Care should be taken not to underestimate what the child can do otherwise the outcomes may reflect the child's lack of response to learning. It may be the case that the child does know how to do something but does not have the ability to express the skills verbally or in certain social situations.

Where possible, targets should be agreed with the pupil and should involve discussions with parents and other professionals.

For children with ASD, targets should also include the treatment and management of any behaviours on which the family or in some cases the child, feel should be focused. An individual behaviour profile (IBP) can be prepared on a separate sheet showing how specific behaviours are to be managed with clear guidelines based on policies for restraint, handling and denial of individual rights. Certain personal, social or independence skills may be regarded by teachers and families as priorities and they will therefore need to be included in the education plan.

The IEP should also give details showing how a child will achieve certain behaviours through programmes of positive intervention. In this way, what is achievable will benefit the child's learning and self-esteem and provide opportunities for them to progress in other areas. The criteria for success will also help teachers and parents to identify whether the target set was appropriate and how the child has responded to learning a particular skill. A termly review may also indicate how the criteria for success can be adapted or altered to ensure that the child can achieve a particular skill.

For a less able child it may be that they have a target to sit and do an activity for five minutes, while for another child it could be that they need to recognise when a lesson has ended and they need to move on to the next subject. In both these situations it will be important that the teacher or LSA provides the appropriate support and resources for the child to achieve these aims, which for the child may be a level of independence that they have not previously had.

Monitoring and Reviewing

Schools will adopt a range of different methods for monitoring and reviewing a child's progress in addition to the annual review of the Statement. Effective record keeping by teachers will be the most important source of information for planning new targets or updating any details about the child's level of functioning. This is also where parents will play a part in providing sound knowledge of their child and where their wishes and feelings can be acknowledged as part of the educational process.

Involving Other Agencies/Pastoral Care

Where a child has additional physical or medical problems, parents and teachers may want to invite other professionals to work with the child so that they can benefit from their advice, particularly in aspects of emotional or behavioural support. For example, a child who has a particular problem with sleeping at night may require some additional resources at home as well as sensitive understanding of the child's ability to attend and respond during school. For severely affected children who engage in a lot of isolated or even disturbed behaviour, a therapeutic environment such as a Snoezelen or White Room or a soft play room can be beneficial. Here, a child can spend time with an adult to enable him or her to respond positively to the adult interaction and sensory experiences offered. Music, massage and movement have significant benefits for reducing anxiety or aggressive behaviour and including these in a child's education plan will help to identify how certain behaviours are being managed. Making use of these approaches can have better learning outcomes for the child who is distressed. They are likely to be more beneficial than a 'time out' situation which may result in the child spending too much time away from the learning environment.

There are some children who, as they get older, develop a heightened awareness of the difficulties they are having with social interaction and they can become withdrawn or display more disturbed behaviour. This can lead on to depression or other psychiatric illnesses. Teachers will need to be aware of children who may be showing specific symptoms of these illnesses and should not just equate 'odd' behaviours with the autism. If they are out of character for the child then these will have to be noted and observations and records kept.

In these instances it may be necessary for the teacher or SENCO to involve other professionals for relevant advice and support for a particular child.

INDIVIDUAL BEHAVIOUR PROFILE

Pupil's name: **Date of Birth:** 10.12.86   **Term/Year:** Autumn 97

Description of behaviour:

Repeating answers to questions more than once and also refusing to ask questions.

Reason for the behaviour:

wants to be sure that he has said the correct answer.

How frequent is the behaviour?:

Repeating answers up to 6 times when asked a question. Refusing to answer questions at least twice a day.

Where does the behaviour occur?:

does this during most lessons and in the playground.

Reinforcements and rewards:

If he answers correctly he is thanked.

Strategy

Use Circle Time to practise answering questions from adults and peers. Include discussions on what it feels like to get things wrong. Before asking the question remind him that he only needs to give the answer once. When he has answered correctly say 'YES' before he repeats himself. If he refuses to answer suggest he writes it.

Staff involved:

Parental involvement:

Review date: Dec 97

Headteacher signature:

INDIVIDUAL BEHAVIOUR PROFILE

Pupil's name: **Date of Birth:** 6.10.91   **Term/Year:** Autumn 97

Description of behaviour:

Spitting.

Reason for the behaviour:

does this when she is asked to do something she doesn't want to or is anxious about trying something new.

How frequent is the behaviour?:

Between 10 - 20 times a day depending on the activity.

Where does the behaviour occur?:

In the classroom, at drinktime or sitting in a group. During planned activities.

Reinforcements and rewards:

is given verbal praise for drinking or sitting in the group. She can then have choice of an activity. She likes books and music.

Strategy

Provide activities which she enjoys or can do. If she spits tell her to get a cloth to clean it up.

If she spits at someone (usually an adult) do not give a verbal response. Give instruction and remain with her through set task or activity.

Provide individual work area.

Staff involved:

Parental involvement:

Review date: Dec 97

Headteacher signature:

EXAMPLE
INDIVIDUAL EDUCATION PLAN

Pupil's name: **Date of Birth:** 10.3.91   **NC year & class:** 2P

Stage 2   **Stage 3**   (Statement)   **Date:** September 97

Nature of pupil's difficulty:

has been diagnosed as autistic. He has some speech which is mostly echoed phrases. He can become aggressive and kick and bite staff when upset. He has severe phobias about food and drinking.

Pupil's strengths:

is developing his reading vocabulary. He likes to sing and has a lovely voice and a good sense of rhythm. He can load a program and use the computer independently. He has a delightful personality and responds well to praise.

Priority areas:

To work independently. To join in the group spontaneously without support. To work in a small group.

Medical/Pastoral arrangements:

SALT:	**EP:**
OT: N/A	**Physiotherapist:** N/A
Social Worker:	**Respite:** None yet.
Other:	

Parental Contributions:

Notes in home/school book and phone calls.

Resources and equipment:

Symbols timetable - individual work schedule. He requires one to one for teaching individual skills.

Pupil Comments:

Monitoring Arrangements:

Annual Review. Termly objectives and summaries. Individual Behaviour Profile and Records.

Review date:

March 98

TERM: SPRING   SUMMER

TARGETS	STRATEGY	REVIEW
Write his name independently.	Tracing over letters of his name. Gently support his arm if necessary.	Achieved. Nov 97
Add and subtract up to 20.	Use multi link cubes for visual recognition.	Achieved with help to keep his attention. Dec 97
Name parts of the body and draw a face.	Use flashcards to match large outline. Sing songs about the body. Trace and copy a picture of a face.	Very good at matching words. Needs some help with ears and hair. Dec 97
Follow a sequence of controlled movements in P.E.	On trampoline, work on seat drop, stand and turn. Encourage imitation of short movement sequence run-jump-hop.	Worked really well this term. Dec 97
Language and Communication: Comprehension: Understand "if ......then" **Expressive:** To give information.	Use symbols of 2 activities. Ask "what did you do?" "where have you been?" questions often.	Achieved. Answers when its an activity he enjoyed. Dec 97
Creative Play To play hide and seek or make a house with other children.	In the soft play room with two other children.	Good interaction - often refers to adult first but follows prompt. Dec 97
Personal and Social Education To put on his shoes and socks independently.	With hand over hand, talk through the activity. Also ask him to find his shoes and socks, eg after P.E.	Can be reluctant to try depending on mood. Dec 97
Behaviour Remain sitting during mealtime and drinktime.	Talk about the food. Sing songs to keep his attention. Make his own drink and wait his turn.	Is better with drinktime but still unsettled at lunch. Dec 97
Teacher responsible:		

EXAMPLE
INDIVIDUAL EDUCATION PLAN

Pupil's name: **Date of Birth:** 6.4.87   **NC year & class:** 4R
Stage 2   **Stage 3**   (**Statement**)   **Date:** September 97

Nature of pupil's difficulty: has been diagnosed as having Asperger syndrome. His eyesight is not good and he wears glasses. Tendency to be a bit clumsy.
Pupil's strengths: Very competent on the computer. Enjoys working with numbers.
Priority areas: Reduce social isolation in the playground and join in class discussions.

Medical/Pastoral arrangements:

SALT:	**EP:**
OT:	**Physiotherapist:**
Social Worker:	**Respite:** None required
Other: Teacher for visually impaired.	

Parental Contributions: Termly meeting and phone calls.
Resources and equipment: Access to computer. 10 hours SSA.
Pupil Comments: says that he doesn't like P.E. because he can't do it.
Monitoring Arrangements: Annual Review.
Review date: April 98

48

TERM: (AUTUMN)   SPRING   SUMMER

TARGETS	STRATEGY	REVIEW
Improve handwriting.	Tracing letters and using guidelines. Remember to praise his efforts.	Worked hard, some improvements. Needs lots of practice. Dec 97
Solving problems involving multiplication and division.	Use practical examples - break down long written questions let him check using the calculator.	Achieved 10 x Oct 97 Manages calculations. Needs help with long problems. Dec 97
To use equipment and power sources safely.	Talk about the equipment. Support with pictures to remind him what to do.	Has a better understanding. Needs watching. Dec 97
To pass a ball to another person, eg throwing and kicking.	Choose one person to work with him. Work on short distances and only briefly. See OT programme.	Occasionally anxious, better 1 : 1 Dec 97
Language and Communication: Comprehension: Describe stories he has heard. **Expressive:** Share conversation.	Help him to make lists of important aspects of the story in role play. Answering questions.	Used computer for this. Needs lots of practice. Dec 97
Creative Play Make up a story with other pupils.	Use a character he is familiar with, eg from the computer.	Liked the idea and was better in the group situation. Dec 97
Personal and Social Education To spend more time in small group work.	Use Circle Time to teach about sharing ideas and conversation.	Enjoyed these. Sessions will be continued next term. Dec 97
Behaviour To accept taking turns to use the computer.	Make a list of children's names so he recognises when it is his turn.	Appreciated the list but got upset when his turn ended. Dec 97
Teacher responsible:		

Whole School Policy

To ensure that the educational needs of children with ASD are being met within their school placement, schools will need to adopt a policy which reflects the aims of their school and acknowledges that such children have very different learning needs to those of their peers. The policy should include:

- an explanation of the autistic disorder and the specific learning needs of these children;
- teaching approaches which benefit children with ASD;
- strategies for the positive management of behaviour;
- the use of resources and special environments to support learning;
- an ongoing programme of staff training.

In setting up such a policy, schools can receive input from the SENCO or an advisory teacher who has a special interest or additional responsibility for monitoring the needs of pupils with ASD.

Further information on setting up IEPs and developing SEN policies in schools can be found in the DfEE publication *The SENCO Guide* (1997).

CHAPTER 8
Approaches to Autistic Spectrum Disorder

It is particularly relevant in the light of proposed changes within our education model to consider how we should plan and provide a curriculum for those with ASD. We should now be looking at teaching approaches which broaden our current understanding of education for all children.

Adopting a more eclectic view acknowledges that individuals can benefit from aspects of different approaches especially where they can have a significant effect on the behaviour and progress of children in the classroom.

Over the years a number of therapies and educational approaches have emerged into the literature and practice of working with those who have autism. In some instances these approaches have established themselves as having a considerable effect on learning outcomes and behaviour whilst others have been viewed with some scepticism as to their long-term effects. This is not to say that the latter will have no relevance towards helping those with ASD as there will be aspects of any approach which can be appropriate. Neither does giving a particular approach a label imply its exclusivity, since the philosophies of many of these therapies already exist within what has been described as educational therapy.

Often it can be difficult to acknowledge new techniques which appear to have little to do with the process of education. There will certainly be some approaches which complement current educational practices whilst others which are clinically based may be providing a different role in terms of treatment.

Not all children with this disorder will respond only to one approach and something that works for one child may not for another. Therapies cannot claim to be a cure for ASD but may provide respite from a particular behaviour, emotional disturbance or language difficulty which an individual is experiencing. Likewise it would be inappropriate to suggest that one particular therapy or approach has succeeded or failed as there will always be a combination of factors which will influence the effectiveness of any treatment, such as the home environment, the response of the adults in the learning situation, the child's health and personality and their own response to the treatment.

The following information has been taken from the NAS publication, *Approaches to Autism* (1994). I have also included those approaches where I have had personal experience through my work with children with ASD and their families.

Aromatherapy

Aromatherapy has been used for centuries in different cultures and is now widely used to aid relaxation and reduce stress. It uses essences from plants, mixed with oil, which are massaged into the body. Each of the different plant essences have different properties and are therefore used to treat different symptoms. The basis for this treatment has no specific scientific foundation but its benefits are widely acknowledged by those who have experienced this therapy. A qualified aromatherapist will be able to recommend a course of treatment and they can also prepare the oils for carers to use at other times. Those who are very emotionally disturbed or hyperactive may respond to a hand, foot or head massage in a quiet room. An opportunity to relax may help to reduce any anxiety and enable them to take part in other planned activities. In this way the experience is a positive one for the individual and for the person working with them. It may be difficult to say when such a session could take place as it may not be possible to have a set time for it to happen. There is also no guarantee that this will reduce any disturbed behaviour. Another area of concern may also be the intimacy of the situation and it may therefore only be appropriate when there are other adults present or it is something which their primary carers can do at home. Care should be taken to use only those oils recommended by an aromatherapist as some can have adverse effects on children, particularly if they suffer from epilepsy. More information can be found at Natural Health Centres or the International School of Aromatherapy based in London.

Auditory Integration Training

Auditory Integration Training was introduced by Dr Guy Berard in the 1960s. The equipment he devised was originally used to assist those with auditory difficulties and was designed to exercise the hearing apparatus. This technique was then used for children with ASD to help reduce the hypersensitivity to sounds from which many of them suffer.

It is an intense programme of auditory sensory stimulation using music which has been especially recorded and modulated to affect changes in the neurological processes. This treatment is only available through private clinics and is generally a treatment which parents will pay for their child to have. Many children with ASD will be hypersensitive to certain sounds and cover their ears to block out sound they do not like. This is because the flow of auditory information is too intense and can be the reason why some children scream or attempt to run away in an attempt to remove what they regard as an unpleasant experience.

Some parents have reported significant improvements in their child's behaviour, which for a family may be very important, others have identified improvements in the development of speech and being able to attend (*The Sound of a Miracle* by A Stehli, 1991, published by Fourth Estate). However, there will be children for whom this therapy is not appropriate and there have been examples where there has been no significant change or worse behaviour emerging. Further information can be found by contacting the Tomatis Centre UK, Lewes, E. Sussex, The Reve Pavilion, Guildford, Surrey or Hale Clinic, London W1N.

Behavioural Intervention - Lovaas

In 1987 Ivar Lovaas reported on an intensive behavioural treatment programme which he had been working on with young children with autism and pervasive developmental disorder. He found that after a programme of intensive behaviour modification over two years the symptoms of autism had diminished enabling them to attend the mainstream school where they were functioning well within their peer group level.

This approach, also known as Applied Behaviour Analysis, aims to modify behaviours by an intensive programme of one-to-one therapy to increase language, attention, imitation, social behaviour, appropriate independent play and decrease any stereotypic, aggressive or ritualist behaviours. The programme is usually started when a child is young, around the age of 2, when they will receive up to 40 hours a week of intensive therapy for at least two years or more if the child has not made sufficient progress.

There are many claims that this approach has 'cured' children of the underlying cognitive difficulties related to autism and this has led to its increased popularity. In a study carried out by Jordan (1991) she queried whether this is actually the case or whether it is the intensity of the programme which helps to raise IQ and reduce the effects of autism, such as poor attention, poor language skills and stereotypic behaviours. What is perhaps more relevant is that this provides an opportunity for parents and carers to be involved in the treatment sessions and this can also have a profound effect on the outcomes.

Whilst many parents are enthusiastic about this approach there are some concerns about aversives and the types of reinforcers used when the child gives an incorrect response. Teachers may also feel that the intense one-to-one therapy provides no opportunity for the child to learn within a social context and this isolation may exacerbate difficulties that the child may have with interaction in later life. The manual for parents and professionals, *Behavioural Intervention for Young Children with Autism*, edited by C. Maurice, published by PRO-ED, provides a comprehensive explanation of the Lovaas method. There are also articles available in the journal, *Autism Research Review International*, which examine further research on this approach.

Daily Life Therapy

Daily Life Therapy was founded by Dr Kitahara in Japan. Her views on the education of children with ASD have largely been advanced at the Higashi school in Boston, USA, where it has gained in its popularity. Daily Life Therapy reflects the eastern philosophy of education based on the stability of the emotions, improved physical strength and stimulation of the intellect. Kitahara believed that those with ASD need to be brought out of their social isolation and through an intensive programme of independence skills, physical activity and academic work the children are encouraged to develop skills in socialisation and communication. Music and art are also emphasised within the programme since they seem to support the development of perceptual awareness, language and socialisation. Children are taught in very structured class groups, learning with a peer group not segregated by ability. The very structured approach which permeates through all their physical, creative, daily living skills and learning activities is seen as a way of controlling any aberrant behaviours and developing cognitive skills which can enable them to function better. Some schools in this country have adopted the physical education programmes used by the Higashi school to enhance the physical and mental functioning in those with ASD. The Higashi approach regards children's learning as occurring predominantly in a social group, which does suggest that there may be reduced opportunities for a child to behave and respond independently. Information and articles on Daily Life Therapy are widely available in journals about special education and these may also have articles written from the parents' perspectives.

Dietary Intervention

The links between diet and behaviour have been discussed by the medical profession since the 1970s. In particular, additives in foods have been found to affect hyperactivity in some children and there is an increasing awareness of food intolerance with other disabilities, eg migraine, asthma, coeliac disease. The research currently being carried out at Sunderland University by Dr Paul Shattock and his colleagues has identified an impaired immune system in those with autism who have abnormally high quantities of peptides in the urine. The effect of this chemical imbalance on the neurotransmitters can subsequently have an effect on pain, mood and perception. Many of the people studied were also experiencing bowel and stomach problems which has led researchers to consider the extent of food intolerances in others with ASD (Waring, 1991).

These studies have also found a number of children with ASD who suffer from the yeast infection, candida albicans, who have benefited from the elimination of yeast and sugar from their diet. There are also those children who are intolerant of foods containing additives and this will be indicated in their behaviour which can be erratic or even aggressive, or a response to pain.

Studies have shown (Reichelt et al, 1990) that many children have an intolerance to gluten and casein (found in milk products) and are unable to break down these proteins, causing them some physiological disturbance. Dietary intervention is only likely to occur where a child is showing particular symptoms of food intolerance and since this may only be one aspect of the autism, it may be difficult to establish the long-term effects of such treatment.

Information about the latest research findings can be obtained from the Autism Research Unit, Sunderland University or through Brenda Reilly, 3, Palmera Avenue, Calcot, Reading, Surrey RG3 7DZ. The Autism Research Institute, San Diego, USA also produces a quarterly journal, Autism Research Review International.

ENABLE (Encouraging a Natural and Better Life Experience)

ENABLE was devised by speech and language therapists to provide a comprehensive programme for developing communication amongst those with learning difficulties and their carers whether this is in the home, the school or the adult day centre. The intervention aims to promote maximum independence, and functional communication by building on a person's strengths within a given location which is familiar to the individual and their carer. The programme is made up of four sections which are inter-related.

It begins with a theory of the dynamics of communication and what is required to facilitate its improvement. It then involves devising a profile of the communication skills of an individual, the group and what is required within the environment which will affect how the person functions within it. Once the profiles have been established, the programme can be developed which will aim to look at the priorities for the individual, the group and the environment. The final section looks at resourcing for these three elements which provide guidelines on facilitating change in basic interaction skills, understanding communication, expressing self, the communication used by carers and communication required to make the environment more accessible. This programme could be particularly relevant when establishing a new classroom with a specific group of children. Ensuring that there is a consistent use of the programme across different environments may, however, be difficult to maintain or record.

Facilitated Communication

Facilitated Communication was developed through the work of Rosemary Crossley and her colleagues in Australia in 1975, although the technique of using letter boards to help those with poor communication and motor skills is not new. Facilitated Communication is an augmented communication system which involves a partner supporting the non-verbal child to communicate using aids or electronic devices. The concept behind this is that the non-verbal child may have the skills to communicate using pictures, symbols or words but because of their physical and emotional difficulties with communication they need to be supported by a facilitator. The child is encouraged to point at what they want and they are given a physical support, hand over hand to assist them. Gradually, as the child becomes more fluent with this method, the physical support is withdrawn so that the facilitator touches the elbow and then the shoulder until the child can make use of the symbols or words to make requests, offer information or have a conversation. Facilitated Communication is not intended to replace other ways of communicating and for this reason may not be appropriate for all non-verbal children. Critics of this method have expressed concerns that the facilitator is influencing the responses the child makes through the physical support. Rather, this approach can be seen as an opportunity to provide the very isolated child with a means to communicate and affect choices in their lives.

There have been a few articles written on this approach which can be found in the Journal of Autism and Developmental Disorders and others dealing with communication impairments in people with disabilities.

Gentle Teaching

John McGee, founder of the Gentle Teaching approach, describes it as an unconditional valuing of the child, their behaviour and their disability. Gentle Teaching is strategy based on the Psychology of Interdependence which emphasises the development of a relationship between the child and the carer. It is a completely non-aversive approach for those with special needs and challenging behaviour which has four primary aims: to teach the person to feel safe, to teach the person to feel engaged with someone, to teach the person to feel unconditionally valued and to teach the person to return the unconditional valuing.

This approach requires the creation of an atmosphere which is not based on compliance and obedience but on mutual interdependence. Any behaviour is responded to with acceptance by the caregiver so that the child learns to reciprocate in a valued relationship with them. Reports of this method suggest that it has been effective in the elimination of aggressive and self-injurious behaviour (McGee, 1998), but it is not certain whether, as a result of the highly dependent nature of the relationship between the child and caregiver, the child is able to function in the same way in less familiar situations.

Intensive Interaction

In their book *Access to Communication*, Nind and Hewett (1994) describe Intensive Interaction as an approach to interaction with non-verbal people based on the interaction techniques used between young infants and their primary caregivers. The early communication skills which young babies are born with means that they soon learn how to get a carer's attention, they recognise that their actions and sounds are responded to and that they can affect the behaviour of their carers by what they do. These skills will either be missing or significantly impaired in the child with ASD and they will need opportunities to practise these skills so that they can develop more meaningful relationships with those around them.

The most important aspect of this approach is that the teacher takes on a different role through their language and tone of voice, and playing games which will interest the child and encourage them to interact. For the child who is constantly seeking out objects to twiddle or mouth, the adult needs to make what they are doing more interesting so that the child moves their attention away from the object to the person near them. Once the adult achieves their attention, there is no set time or set activities which need to be achieved but the child and adult work intuitively together making use of facial expressions, noises and games involving anticipation and turn taking.

This approach is about seeking quality in a relationship so that the person can learn that interacting with others can affect what happens to them. Intensive Interaction has no specific relevance to a curriculum model but this should in no way undervalue the role that it can play in developing meaningful interaction. After all, there will be no incentive for a child to learn if he or she cannot relate his or her learning to the responses he or she gains from others.

Mediated Learning Experience

According to Feuerstein (1991) 'children do not have low IQs but cognitive deficiencies which create an impairment of learning.' Feuerstein, an Israeli psychologist, developed three educational philosophies which have formed the basis of his work with learning impaired children. Firstly, there is the Mediated Learning Experience which is based on the quality of interaction between the child and the mediator enabling the child to develop different ways of thinking so that learning can take place. He believes that through this positive interaction with a mediator, a child has the ability to develop greater flexibility and adapt to different stimuli and information, thus enhancing their cognitive structures, or intelligence.

Secondly, Feuerstein devised a programme of Instrumental Enrichment which helps students to establish the cognitive foundations of learning. It is a classroom curriculum which is designed to be used for two or three years. Through trained mediators, it aims to help them develop the skills, concepts, strategies and techniques to become independent learners so that they gain a better understanding of their own thinking skills.

Thirdly, the Learning Propensity Assessment Device is a cognitive assessment which evaluates the propensity for cognitive development. It is a series of tests and activities which evaluate the development of cognitive functions and identify the way in which an individual learns. Rather than recording scores this device uses observation to assess how the individual is solving problems.

It may be possible to recognise the Mediated Learning Experience as one of the ways many people are working with children with ASD. The nature of the disorder implies that those working with them will be constantly creating new experiences and positive ways to relate to the child so that the learning can occur.

The detailed assessments devised by Feuerstein form a major part of the work with children who have a learning disability. However, they may be difficult to carry out since there are few people in this country currently trained in the use of this method. More information about this approach can be obtained from the Hadassah-Wizo-Canada Research Institute, Jerusalem, Israel.

Megavitamin Therapy

Research has been carried out for a number of years which has examined the effects of drugs on reducing many features of autism thought to be caused by allergies or brain chemical abnormalities (Rimland, 1993).

It has also sought explanations for the damage to the neuro-chemical pathways affecting the language delay, aggression, self-injury and the obsessional and ritualistic behaviours found in many children and adults with autism and pervasive developmental disorder. The use of megadoses of vitamins such as vitamin B6 and magnesium have been found to improve behaviours in groups of people with ASD during studies (Rimland, 1994). Studies by Dr Waring (1991) at Birmingham University have shown that where there is an inability to break down the enzymes and sulphur compounds. These become toxins in the body which cause a metabolic imbalance. Providing high doses of multivitamins and mineral supplements aims to detoxify the neuro and digestive systems. In one group studied, there have been some improvements in reducing symptoms of hyperactivity, intense craving or dislike of certain foods, excessive sweating or thirst, a pale complexion, irritable bowel syndrome and petit mal or absences which were all symptoms of food and chemical intolerances.

The megavitamin approach to treatment has created a lot of debate about the uses of drug therapy since it has not always been possible to ascertain whether lower levels of certain enzymes relate specifically to those with ASD. Consequently the long-term effects are not yet fully understood especially in terms of any adverse side effects. The Autism Research Review International provides up-to-date information on all research relating to megavitamin therapy.

Music, Art and Movement Therapy

Music therapy has already been mentioned as an approach widely used in many schools for children with learning difficulties. Music is seen as a way of developing communication through using instruments, encouraging the child to engage in 'conversations' with different musical sounds with the adult following the child's early attempts to initiate a two-way conversation. Lists of qualified music therapists can be obtained from the British Society for Music Therapists.

Art therapy is also a valuable form of expression for those with little or no language. The therapist aims to work with an individual, recognising their skills and developing their work from the child's interests. Art can reflect moods and emotions and pictures are created with the therapist working in an empathetic role through art. Children's interests and obsessions can also be used during these sessions so that if a child likes one particular colour they can paint or use materials in this colour to create something which they can enjoy looking at. Another child may be interested in lines and enjoy making patterns which the therapist can then use to talk to the child about the shapes they are making. Some children delight in exploring different materials through tactile experiences which again can be provided so that the child can relate to the positive experience.

Because many children with ASD can have very poor motor coordination, movement therapy can help them to develop greater spatial and physical awareness. Posture, awareness of personal space, lack of awareness of physical strength and erratic movements can be addressed through a movement session enabling the child to develop a greater sense of themselves and how they move in relation to others. Like all the therapies mentioned here, it is also about communicating, either with a therapist or a partner, so that movements can initiate contact, be imitated or extended to create a spontaneous interaction with another person.

Veronica Sherborne (1990) devised a way of working with children who have a range of physical and mental disabilities. Sherborne Movement, as it is now called, focuses not only on teaching physical skills but on developing an awareness of self and others. In a one-to-one situation, the child works through a series of movements with their 'carer' which involve trust (for example, supporting); security (containing as in rocking); developing confidence (crawling); and relaxation (being still or rolling).

Through these shared creative experiences there is an opportunity for developing a sense of relating to others and it is the quality of this interaction which aims to help them to develop greater confidence and self-esteem. They can therefore be relevant to anyone with a mental or psychiatric disorder or physical impairment.

The Son Rise Programme - Options

The Options philosophy was begun by the Kaufmans following the treatment they gave to their son who was diagnosed as being autistic. The Options Institute in Massachusetts provides a comprehensive programme to support the child with ASD and helps the parents to have a better understanding of how to affect change in the behaviour of the person with ASD. The book *Son-Rise: The Miracle Continues* by Barry Neil Kaufman, provides insight into how this programme has developed and how other families have used the programme.

Initially the child is placed in a room with a therapist who attempts to play with the child responding positively to anything that the child does. The approach works on the premise that everyone has a choice about how they feel and what they do and that doing enjoyable things makes us want to find out more, thus we adapt our behaviour to make this happen. For parents coping with a diagnosis of ASD they may not have been able to recognise this and subsequently they may feel uncertain about how to interact with their child. One of the positive features of the Options approach is the way in which it involves the parents and trains them to work with their child. The person working with the child has to adopt a complete acceptance of the child, not seeing them as someone with a disability but as someone who has a right to show any emotion or behave in any way that they want. In this way they see the child as being freed from their isolated state and learning to have some control rather than feeling that the world is always controlling them.

Like the Lovaas method the intervention is very intensive and for this reason it can be said to have an effect on improving the child's responses. Although the learning appears to be more child centred, there are certainly elements of behaviour modification being used especially with regards to the responses given by the adult who will 'play down' or ignore the stereotypic behaviours while praising the good things that the child is doing. It is not yet clear what the long-term benefits of this approach actually are but it does appear to be a more positive way of gaining the child's interest rather than where the adult is always controlling the learning. The Options Institute, Massachussetts, USA, can provide additional information and articles written about this approach.

PECS (Picture Exchange Communication System)

PECS was developed by Andrew Bondy and Lori Frost in Delaware, USA. It is a structured programme designed to encourage communication skills in young children with ASD and those with other disabilities who have not developed functional communication.

PECS is based on using pictures to enable the child to direct communication to others. It is particularly relevant for those with autism who have good visual understanding and the child soon realises that they can use the pictures to make requests for things that they want. PECS also provides them with a visual cue to interact which can aid their attention and lessen their need to resort to a behaviour outburst. Consequently they can soon learn that there will be a positive response to their attempts to interact. The carer or therapist offers the child a picture and the child then chooses from their set of pictures what they want. In this way they are able to make choices rather than always having to be directed.

The effectiveness of this programme has been that it overcomes difficulties some children have with signing and pointing and has aided the development of speech much earlier than under these other systems. It has also been effective in terms of developing early communication skills in preschool children as it can be used in the home. The authors of this approach have also recognised that it fits well into other programmes such as Portage, TEACCH and applied behaviour analysis. Information about this approach can be obtained from the Speech and Language Therapy Service.

Psychotherapy

The use of psychotherapy in the treatment of ASD has a historical basis since it was thought that the behaviours that these children were displaying were a result of some psychological disturbance due to child rearing practices. Treatment was focused on the family by looking at how behaviours could be changed through improved relationships between the family members. Follow-up studies on the effectiveness of psychotherapy (Creak, 1963; Eisenburg, 1956, 1957a; Kanner, 1973) found no specific benefits of this treatment for the primary impairments of ASD and subsequent studies (Schopler, 1966) acknowledged that the underlying causes of the autistic disorder do not respond well to this type of treatment (cited in Wing, *Early Childhood Autism*, p.298, 1976).

Where psychotherapy may be helpful is in working with families, addressing some of the feelings arising from the prolonged impaired relationships and the effects on the siblings of having a person with ASD in the family. Some children and young adults with ASD may find psychotherapy helpful if they are experiencing some disturbance around issues of coping or managing independently. It is no longer likely to be provided as a means of identifying some of the underlying causes of the disorder. Counselling and practical support are probably the most effective ways now used to help those with ASD to adapt and learn skills for coping with some of the secondary handicaps associated with the disorder.

TEACCH (Treatment and Education of Autistic and Related Communication-Handicapped Children)

In 1966 Professor Eric Schopler set up Division TEACCH at the University of North Carolina. It was designed to be a comprehensive, community-based service for those with autism and their families. It established a clinical diagnostic service and extended services to support children in their schools. It has been responsible for setting up classroom programmes, residential programmes and vocational programmes as well as ongoing research and training.

The educational methods are based on:

- improving skills by education and modifying the environment to accommodate deficits
- parent collaboration
- assessment for individualised programmes
- structured teaching
- enhancing skills by recognising their strengths and focusing on emerging skills
- cognitive and behaviour therapy
- training professionals in all aspects of teaching children with autism

(*Approaches to Autism*, NAS, 1993)

This child centred approach gave rise to the specific methods of teaching which involve planning the physical organisation of the classroom, timetabling activities so that the child knows what is going to happen and preparing activities and teaching materials using visual and written cues.

The philosophy underlying this is that by making the environment more predictable, the child is less confused and behaviour problems will be reduced. It also acknowledges that children with ASD learn best on an individual basis rather than in groups and the teaching style will reflect this. Children are given individual work areas where they work through a series of set tasks which they can complete independently. New skills are taught on a one-to-one basis and rehearsed frequently by the child to help them to consolidate what they have learnt.

Assessments are the vital factor in planning what a child needs to learn since through these the teacher can ascertain a child's individual strengths and any emerging skills.

Both the CARS (Childhood Autism Rating Scale) and the PEP-R (Psychoeducational Profile Revised) provide a detailed assessment of the child. In addition they also help to identify how the child responds to learning, ie their motivation, distractibility and attention span. The learning objectives for each child are then determined by the following criteria:

developmental appropriateness
functionality
independence
coordination with parental priorities and practices

The popularity of TEACCH has probably been its emphasis on early intervention programmes, with parents and other therapists working in collaboration throughout the person's life. It also recognises that there is a whole spectrum of support required which is based on individual needs and therefore its application can be advocated in a range of educational settings. Many LEAs and schools have set up TEACCH training courses and literature about this approach has become more widely available in recent years. Further information can also be obtained from the NAS.

CHAPTER 9
Which Educational Placement?

Following the statutory assessments the LEA will, in discussion with parents, make proposals for the most appropriate placement for a child. This could mean a child having a special school placement or remaining in a mainstream school with a programme of learning support. If it is felt that a child's present mainstream environment will not be able to provide the necessary resources to support the child's learning then an alternative placement will be sought. Deciding on an appropriate placement can be difficult for parents as they will want to be sure that the school can adequately support their child and understand the specific difficulties which the child is experiencing.

The majority of children with ASD will require specialist teaching whether this is in a special school or mainstream school. It is likely that in schools where a child is placed, staff will develop an understanding of ASD or have specialist knowledge about the education of children with this disorder. In some cases a team of professionals will be working closely with the school to devise and implement an education plan for a child and this will help to support the way in which the teacher is managing the child in the class.

Playgroups and Nursery Schools

Very young children attending a playgroup or nursery school are likely to be identified early on as having special educational needs. The child will probably have a significant language delay or if they are talking it may be very repetitive or pedantic speech. Also their behaviour may be bizarre and unpredictable and this can have significant implications for their management. The focus on learning through play for children in this age group may also highlight some of the problems which children with ASD have in developing symbolic or imaginative skills. Other children in the playgroup may find the child's behaviour disturbing and staff may find it difficult to gain a child's attention or encourage them to take part in a task or group activity.

It may be helpful to discuss with parents how they manage certain behaviours to help reduce stressful situations for the child and provide consistency in the way his or her behaviour is managed. The child may also have particular likes and dislikes or even phobias about certain situations which may upset the child and cause disturbance. Something as simple as a toy could frighten the child because of the noise it makes.

If staff are concerned as a result of any difficulties which the child is having within the playgroup or nursery they can, having discussed this with parents, seek further support from health or education professionals.

Following an early diagnosis most preschool children will attend an assessment unit attached to a Child Development Centre based at a hospital where they can benefit from having early input from other health professionals. More severely affected children can also attend a nursery based in a special school which will offer early intervention to encourage their social and communication skills.

C attends the local nursery school three mornings a week. C has a support worker assigned to work with her. C had no speech but would occasionally make noises of things she had heard from the television. Initially C was unhappy about being left and spent most of her time in the book corner where staff found it difficult to get her to do anything else. She did not relate well to staff and when they tried to get her to join in she would scream, so staff tended to leave her. She would occasionally wander around and pick up a

---

toy but not do anything with it, then put it down and wander off again. The teacher spoke to the mother and it was then decided to try and get some support to work with C. The mother also informed the teacher of things that the child liked doing such as looking at books and playing with water. Once the support worker came she would sit with C in the book corner and encourage her to look at books with her. This helped to develop their relationship and from this C would then spend more time at the different activities. She did not relate to the other children except when she saw a toy she wanted and took it from them but would sit at the table with the other children at drink time. C responded well to music and would happily sit with an instrument during music time and although she did not use words she would try and sing the tunes of familiar songs.

Mainstream Schools

In most cases children with Asperger syndrome or 'higher functioning' autism will have a placement in the mainstream school. These children have significantly better skills in language and have an average or above average intelligence. This can be very misleading in terms of early assessments which may not take into account how much they are understanding and how they will relate the skills they have for working in social situations with other children. Consequently learning support can vary and will depend on the individual needs of the child, the school policy on supporting children with SEN and the classroom organisation. They may have an assistant with them for certain lessons or times of the day, or they may go to a resource base within the school to work. In some cases they may not require any learning support because they are functioning well within the structure the class is providing and the school has made the necessary arrangements to support the child's social and personal development.

Ensuring that the child has access to the National Curriculum may require some adaptations to the way in which the work or information is presented with additional resources and teaching materials required to make it easier for them to grasp a particular concept or skill. The teacher, who will be working closely with the assistant, will ensure that the child is working towards the targets set out in the IEP. The assistant will also develop a good knowledge of the child recognising when they can manage more independently and in what areas they need specific support.

Many children will also benefit from an individual behaviour profile (IBP) highlighting difficult areas of behaviour and strategies for managing the behaviour which have been negotiated between the pupil and the teacher. The child may be aware of situations and problems which give rise to a behaviour outburst but not always be able to plan to keep away from the source of the problem. This can often be the case with social situations where they may want to try and make friends but not recognise bullying or teasing as an unfriendly response.

Some LEAs have also included children with ASD who are less able into the mainstream school setting because of a policy of having no segregated education. These children are likely to receive much higher levels of support with a full-time class assistant and have regular input from other professionals such as an occupational therapist or a speech and language therapist.

Schools which have a policy of full integration for pupils with SEN will have developed an approach to the curriculum which acknowledges the different learning styles of children with special educational needs within the mainstream classroom. This is likely to go hand in hand with the constant need for schools to foster an ethos of care and respect for all its pupils.

Whilst it is important that children are given every opportunity to learn with their peer group it may not always be easy for the other children to understand why a child is behaving in a certain way, especially when their attempts at being sociable may not be responded to in a way they would expect.

Transition from primary to secondary education can also pose significant problems. Where the child has been used to the smaller, more intimate environment of the primary school, they then have to adjust to moving to classes for different subjects and being taught by different teachers when they go to secondary school. The level of pastoral care within the secondary environment will need to be carefully planned. On the one hand the child may not take too kindly to being shadowed by an adult all the time which may highlight the fact that they are different to the other pupils. It can also happen that a child is placed in a class for low achievers because they are seen as needing additional support. This could be very frustrating for a child who is academically quite able and recognises that they are being put with less able children. As a result the child may experience further emotional and behaviour problems in an attempt to express their underlying concerns.

R attends the local village primary school where he is in a class of 24 pupils in Years 1 and 2. He has a special support assistant for 15 hours a week and this time is planned with the teacher so that she is with him for the morning and part of the afternoon. R has a good reading vocabulary but has difficulty understanding what he is reading. The class assistant has individual time with him helping him with his reading and working on comprehension where he completes worksheets prepared by the teacher. In addition to working through his maths programme she also runs through his hand exercises, planned by the OT to encourage his hand function and fine motor skills. Currently R has access to all the subjects in the National Curriculum and clearly benefits from the additional support he receives. R is now more willing to join in whole class activities such as story time, usually because he gets the chance to choose the book. However, he does find assemblies difficult and will sometimes make noises and have to be taken out of the hall. R is generally making good progress and his parents are keen for him to remain at the school.

Schools for Children with Emotional and Behaviour Difficulties (EBD)

There are a small minority of children with ASD who have been given a placement in a school for children with emotional and behavioural difficulties because their behaviour was regarded in the mainstream setting as disruptive or deviant. Such a placement may have occurred where a child had not had a diagnosis of ASD which would account for some of the behaviours the child was displaying. Generally the underlying cause for the behaviour difficulties is not the same as those of their peers in the EBD school and this might cause further problems for the child. They may feel vulnerable in a situation which they cannot manage and resort to certain behaviours as a way of avoiding a difficult social experience. In some instances the different teaching approaches have had benefits for the child with ASD where they may be able to learn strategies for coping with aspects of their behaviour. However, a mainstream placement should continue to be an option for the child.

Special Units or Classes

There will be some children who are attending a unit or Special Support Facility (SSF) for those with language and communication disorders attached to a mainstream school. These units will support children who have a range of different language disorders but may well have a few children within the autistic spectrum who will require specific understanding of their language and communication difficulties. There will be a stronger emphasis on developing language and communication skills with resources and materials designed to support all aspects of the curriculum. Children may spend some time in the mainstream classroom but also withdraw for certain sessions where they can have specialised individual attention. I have observed one such facility where children from the mainstream classrooms can also go into the special class for certain lessons to enable those with language or communication difficulties to work in small social groups.

O attends an SSF for children with language and communication difficulties which is based in a primary school. O has Asperger syndrome and a mild visual impairment. O spends the morning in the SSF where he has an individual programme to work through. He also receives speech therapy on two mornings during the week and the class assistant continues his programme at other times. The teacher tries to ensure that O spends time with other children in the mainstream classroom for one lesson a day but the teacher of this class reports that O tends to stay by himself and does not make much contact with the other children. O needs an adult observing him when he is in the playground as he will swear at other children when they will not let him join in with their games.

Schools for Children with Moderate Learning Difficulties (MLD)

Children with ASD in these schools will be functioning at an intellectual level similar to their peer group and show some ability with language and social skills. Most children will be able to fit into the subject-based curriculum but may still have significant difficulties with aspects of social communication and processing information.

Some aspects of their learning may need to be taught in very small steps especially in the areas of personal and social development and independence skills. It may be necessary to provide specific programmes and at times, opportunities for individual teaching to consolidate those skills.

In some schools there may also be a specialist class for children with ASD who are within the MLD range of ability but who require a specific environment in which to learn. These classes will probably be run by a teacher who has specialist knowledge of autistic spectrum disorder and there will be a higher staff/pupil ratio than there is in the rest of the school.

D has Asperger syndrome and is now in the secondary department of the MLD school. He copes well with the subject-based curriculum and has no problems getting around the school as he has been at the school since primary age. Both he and his teachers have recognised that his biggest difficulty is in getting himself organised for his lessons, doing his homework and keeping his notes tidy. D hopes to take some GCSEs. His favourite activity is working on the computer and given the chance he would do nothing else. His parents are trying to work with the school to make sure he does his homework before being allowed time on the computer at home.

Schools for Children with Severe Learning Difficulties (SLD)

Since the majority of children with ASD will have severe learning difficulties an appropriate placement in an SLD school will provide a developmental curriculum relevant to the level at which they are functioning. These children may display more difficult behaviours requiring very specific behaviour programmes, or they may have an additional handicap which is also affecting their general development and behaviour. A developmental curriculum focuses on early language and cognitive skills and will have tasks broken down into much smaller steps to enable the child with severe learning difficulties to assimilate the skills they need for learning. The developmental curriculum fits into the National Curriculum with a series of phases or attainments which a child with SLD can achieve to work towards the National Curriculum Key Stages.

Often these children are placed in a class group with children who have other physical and mental disabilities and therefore the extent to which these children are likely to interact with their peers may be considerably impaired given the nature of the disabilities of others in the class. A classroom which is designed to stimulate and encourage pupils to learn using a wide variety of stimulus materials and visually attractive displays can be distracting and sometimes disturbing for children with ASD and this may make it more difficult for them to access the curriculum. Some schools have set up classrooms specifically for this group of children, based on a high level of structure and using resources and teaching methods which are more relevant to their learning needs.

S has ASD and is in a class of Year 1 and 2 pupils with a range of different disabilities including those with profound learning difficulties. Initially in this class S was very aggressive and hyperactive. He disliked any efforts made to interact with him other than on his terms and he would kick out if he was expected to join in with an activity he did not want to. S had some language which was very repetitive and he only spoke in echoed phrases. Within a short space of time S was responding to symbols and relied on these to identify which activities he was doing each day. He has a very structured individual programme of work and staff consistently manage his behaviour. S has been learning to read and write and he has a natural aptitude and interest in numbers and has progressed well in these subjects. Learning to read has also helped to develop his language which he now uses to offer information. His aggressive outbursts are much less frequent and he can join in with a group activity if it is something he enjoys, such as music. S has made attempts to interact with his peers but prefers to watch the older children in the playground and tries to join in with them. He also has very significant eating and drinking phobias and there has been close liaison with home to establish ways of reducing this.

Specialist Schools

A small number of children will attend a specialist school for children with ASD or language impairments run by a local Autistic Society, the National Autistic Society or a private organisation. These schools may be some distance from the child's home and may offer residential or day placements. For some children and their families there is a need for the child to receive a 24-hour curriculum so that learning is consistent in all aspects of their daily living. There will be some children who are so severely affected that they require a very sympathetic and therapeutic learning environment with a high level of care and support.

A preferable residential placement could be for weekly boarding so that the child can spend time with the family at the weekends or it can be run on short-term breaks so that contact with the family is maintained. The parents may also have chosen such a placement because they feel that their child has significantly fallen behind in their acquisition of skills in the mainstream or special school environment. They may consider that in this type of school their child will benefit from the specialized approaches and understanding of the disability which will support their child's learning.

P has ASD and when younger she displayed many behaviours which her parents found very difficult to manage. Family outings were always a trauma as she would scream if she did not want to be in a certain place and try and run away. The family found it increasingly difficult to go out together. At home she would wander around the house and never settle to anything and would only sit at mealtimes. Her parents had found it difficult to toilet train her and when wearing pads she would try to shred these. Both the parents and the school approached the education authority to consider a residential placement for her.

Even though the parents found her difficult to manage they were not really happy about her going away from home but were prepared to accept this would be the best situation for P and the family. P has benefited from the 24-hour curriculum the school offers and boarding weekly means that she goes home to the family at weekends. The school reports that she is progressing well, has learnt Makaton signing and uses symbols to communicate. She has also managed to go without pads and her parents find that she is good about using the toilet at home too. Now when she is home the parents choose to do activities which they know she likes, such as walking in the countryside.

Private Schools

Some parents may decide to send their child to a private school where there are smaller class groups and the opportunity for the child to receive more individual attention within a normal class setting.

There have been a few cases where an LEA has jointly funded such a placement or has made provision for some additional class support if it is considered to be the most appropriate placement for the child.

Inclusion or Segregation?

Having briefly touched on how some children with ASD will be included within the mainstream classroom, it would be appropriate to consider some of the benefits and disadvantages of such provision, particularly as it may affect the placements of some children in the future.

With our current education model children with ASD, whether or not they have had a diagnosis, are likely to have a placement in a school which is based on their level of intellectual functioning. My own observation in one LEA has identified children in different educational settings where this is not necessarily the case. These children tended to have placements where their needs were met in terms of the management of their behaviour, the additional staff/pupil ratios and specialist resources, or because of parental preferences.

An inclusive model could be seen as a way of removing such discrepancies, enabling all children to have the same educational opportunities which are differentiated to meet individual needs. It is also a model which moves towards a child-based rather than an instruction-based curriculum. Parental involvement and a programme of staff training would also play a large part in the success of such a placement especially in helping to develop greater understanding of the child within the school community.

There are those professionals and parents who would question whether the majority of children with ASD would fit well into this model of provision, since it is now recognised that the educational needs of children with this disorder are qualitatively different to those of any other group of children with special educational needs. Those who are placed in mainstream environments will require a considerable amount of resourcing in terms of staffing and access to other professionals, additional equipment and adaptations to the curriculum and this could be seen as having a negative effect on the learning needs of the rest of the children in the school.

Alternatively, some professionals have considered whether segregated classes are appropriate for teaching social and communication skills since children with ASD are less likely to interact with each other because of the impairments they have in these areas. For some children, that specialist environment can be the key for them to be given relevant experiences which will help them to manage in other social situations.

The ethos of any school in relation to the social and moral development of its pupils will provide a framework for supporting those children who have greater difficulties with social interaction. Staff will need to respect that there will be times when children with ASD do have difficulties with interaction and that the school may need to put in place resources to enable them to cope more effectively.

In recent years there has been a development in specialist provision for this group of children and many education authorities have set up units or special classes within mainstream, MLD or SLD schools. Headteachers may also have identified a class group of children who would benefit from a particular teaching approach and subsequently planned a class base within the school. This is an approach to inclusive education which may be more preferential for this particular group of children. A placement in such a unit or class would ensure that the learning needs of these children are being acknowledged in terms of the strategies used and the structured nature of the classroom environment. At the same time they can provide opportunities for them to access other resources within the wider school environment where they can share activities with their peers in meaningful ways.

For those in secondary schools a resource base may provide a place for a pupil to go for certain lessons or at particular times of the day to avoid situations which may be stressful for them.

From a survey carried out in three LEAs (Sussex Autistic Society, 1997) there was evidence to suggest that provision for these children remains patchy and in some cases there was a failure to acknowledge the children's difficulties in terms of their autism and thus provide appropriate placements for them.

What is perhaps most important when looking at the whole spectrum of the disorder, is that there should be access to a range of provision which is best suited to the needs of the individual child and the expectations of the parents.

CHAPTER 10
Staff Training Opportunities

The information in this book has focused on the specific learning needs of those with ASD and suggests that what is required is an approach to teaching a curriculum which is not entirely subject-based. The effectiveness of any training will depend on the knowledge and understanding of the disorder within the particular situation in which staff are working. Whilst it also has to be recognised that teaching approaches will vary according to the children in the school, the basic principles which can be applied should be reflected in a training programme. Most training programmes will identify the broad spectrum of abilities of this group of children and this is where a whole school policy on staff development will enable those working with them to keep up to date with current thinking and practices.

A Training Model
So that staff feel more competent in how they work with children with ASD a training programme will need to include:

- an understanding of the nature of the disorder;
- an explanation of the learning difficulties of children with ASD;
- the specific language difficulties of children with ASD and how they differ from normal language acquisition;
- the cognitive and psychological explanations of the autistic disorder;
- the management of behaviour;
- planning the learning environment and the curriculum;
- strategies for effective teaching;
- policies on the integration of pupils;
- how to assess pupils and write individual education plans;
- monitoring and reporting progress;
- working with parents and professionals;
- therapeutic approaches which support children's learning.

In the following paragraphs I have identified how these components may be addressed and the reasons for their inclusion.

Understanding ASD
Research into the autistic disorder has played a valuable role in informing professionals about the nature of autism and it has also been responsible for the development of many of the educational practices currently available for working with such children (Mesibov, 1986). The medical developments in diagnosis and assessment have provided greater liaison between professionals.

Despite different opinions about the causality of the disorder, teachers and carers are predominantly interested in how a child's learning difficulties will affect their development (Howlin & Rutter, 1987). Teachers will want to consider how they can plan the curriculum to ensure that the skills the child needs will reflect his or her abilities and their response to learning. A teacher who is uncertain of the curriculum content for an individual child may need to adopt other approaches which will be more appropriate.

Identifying the Learning Difficulties
The development of language and communication skills will be a priority for all these children and a training programme will focus on the whole range of skills which these

children need to acquire. The complexities of social communication and the use of non-verbal as well as verbal communication are skills which many people take for granted. Learning about the development of normal language acquisition helps to identify those elements of language in which those with autism may have particular difficulties. Studying the extent of language use and linguistic understanding in people with ASD will therefore be particularly relevant.

Theoretical Approaches to ASD

Explanations of ASD cannot be viewed only in terms of pathology since the cognitive and psychological explanations have also provided considerable insight into the thought processes of people with ASD (Baron-Cohen et al., 1985). The difficulties children with ASD have with memory skills, problem solving, perception, attention and generalising, all have a profound influence on learning outcomes. Recognising the difficulties an individual child is experiencing can have significant implications for teaching through a subject-based curriculum.

Behaviour Management

Responding to behaviour will require a very individual approach. Even in classes where there is more than one child with ASD, the management of behaviour will be dependent on the child's individual responses to their learning environment and how they relate to their peers and the adults in the class. A training programme will help staff to identify the antecedents of the behaviour and how to plan strategies to help to reduce or resolve it. Whilst it may be possible to plan specific strategies for certain occurrences there will be some behaviours, such as those requiring restraint, where there are very specific legal guidelines which will need to be understood. Included in a training programme should be opportunities to plan a whole school behaviour policy and effective team work. Even when working on an individual basis, the need for consistency amongst the adults working with the child is the one factor likely to create the most effective positive outcome.

Teaching Strategies

School-based curriculum development will ensure that all children whether or not they have a disability will have appropriate access to the curriculum and the resources they need to enable them to reach their learning potential. For children with ASD the most effective resource is likely to be the learning environment and the positive approaches devised to teach such children. Expensive equipment will be of little use if the child is unable to access it appropriately or has not been taught the necessary skills to make use of it. Training courses will place considerable emphasis on planning the learning environment and the adaptation and application of different teaching materials. Likewise the curriculum will be of no value to the child if it is presented purely in terms of knowledge acquisition. Balancing the needs of the child with their entitlement to the curriculum should ensure that they are given a broader range of experiences, and this is particularly relevant for those in the lower ability range.

Policies on the Education of Children with ASD

Because children with ASD will be found within the whole range of educational settings opportunities for them to integrate with their peers may also vary. Some LEAs have clear policies on the integration of pupils with special educational needs and in other situations it may be that schools have developed links to enable some children to share in certain activities. When writing a policy on integration it will need to have a clear plan, stating the reasons for integration, how it is to be implemented, managed and recorded and who it will benefit. This again will have to be relevant to the individual child, otherwise an inappropriate placement may result in labelling the child rather than the experience as having failed.

Assessment, Planning and Monitoring

Many teachers and SENCOs now recognise the value of assessments, planning and recording information about individual children. If these are going to be specific for children with ASD then the emphasis will need to be on their levels of communication, and their social and independence skills, rather than just on their cognitive abilities. Assessments based purely on academic achievements can either under- or overestimate an individual's skills and they will not be as effective for planning future provision and resources. How teachers monitor progress will also help to establish the priorities for the child which may not be specific to the National Curriculum but are nonetheless significant to his or her future development.

Liaison with Parents and Professionals

Those living and working with children with ASD will know how their behaviours and responses to learning can change from day to day and not for any particular reason. There may also be a deterioration in skills previously learnt or something a child could do is no longer the case. All these aspects can give those working with them the feeling that they are doing something wrong even if they have competently achieved things with the child in other areas. Staff will need to feel supported in what they are doing and training courses can provide an opportunity to discuss any areas of mutual concern. Staff should also feel able to share these issues with the senior management team, the advisory and support service, or the education psychology service. Opportunities to meet regularly to discuss the effectiveness or otherwise of different approaches can also be a reassurance to staff about the work that they are doing.

Approaches to Autism

A broad overview of the range of approaches which have been devised for working with children with ASD is particularly relevant especially as many of these can be adapted within the classroom setting. A critical appraisal of their effectiveness will also be an important component of any discussion on the different approaches to ASD. As professionals this will help to inform our work and current practices in teaching.

Additional Information

There is now a considerable list of publications available on the subject of ASD. The National Autistic Society has a range of books, articles and journals available to purchase covering many different aspects of caring for and educating children. Other information can be found on the Internet which also includes lists of publications, journals, particular topics relating to autism and useful addresses.

Qualifications and Courses

Currently there is one distance learning course available at the University of Birmingham for an Advanced Certificate or MA in Autism. Many colleges and institutes of higher education may also run specified courses as part of the GNVQ, Open College studies or as a module within an MA or BEd programme. More localised training may be organised by local education authorities usually in response to the growing interests of teachers and other professionals wanting to develop their skills in teaching children with ASD.

Professional and Voluntary Organisations

Those interested in working with children with ASD may also benefit from membership of various professional or voluntary associations such as NASEN, BILD, British Psychological Society, NAS or a local Autistic Society. There are also national and local conferences and courses organised by other professional bodies. These may focus on specific subjects or approaches related to autism or special educational needs and may be of some value in applying certain principles in the classroom.

Conclusion

Working with children with ASD does require teachers to rethink many of the ways they are used to working with children. Teachers will have to consider how they organise the classroom and how they are delivering the curriculum while at the same time recognising the behaviours and emotions which can affect the responses of the child with ASD. It is this aspect of teaching these children which can make it both challenging, frustrating and demanding as well as inspiring. It can also present the teacher with new opportunities to develop different practices to give those with ASD a better entitlement to an education in its broadest sense.

Glossary of Associated Disabilities

Allergy-Induced Autism. Allergies to foods and chemicals which can cause a metabolic imbalance and result in children displaying autistic behaviour.

Angelman's Syndrome. Those affected will have severe or profound learning difficulties. There is a developmental delay in communication skills and social interaction. They have motor difficulties and may be delayed in walking. Often they are overexcitable and can display frequent attacks of giggling. These children will also have epilepsy.

Anoxia. Lack of oxygen to the brain during birth which can result in brain damage.

Attention Deficit/Hyperactive Disorder. Typically they are inattentive, overactive and display a lot of impulsive behaviour. There is a strong genetic cause but also a range of environmental causes such as intolerance to certain foods or toxic and infective agents affecting them during pregnancy.

Candida Albicans. This is a yeast infection, predominantly affecting the gut but resulting in thrush. It is caused by excessive use of antibiotics which diminish the enzyme which prevents the growth of thrush. It can give rise to stomach and bowel problems if it remains untreated and certain foods can make the symptoms worse.

Dyspraxia. Developmental dyspraxia is evident in childhood and describes children who have no obvious physical disabilities but appear clumsy and ill-coordinated. They can also have indistinct or hesitant speech. The cause is thought to be due to damage to the brain with the symptoms presented in different degrees of severity. Their difficulties may become more evident as they get older which can result in them underachieving in certain areas at school. It can also affect their self-esteem and they may behave in negative ways. Some may become socially isolated and depressed because they are ridiculed by their peers.

Encephalitis. Inflammation of the brain caused by viral or bacterial infections. There is residual brain damage and behaviour problems.

Fragile X. Affects the whole range of ability. Males tend to have more autistic behaviours, be overactive and impulsive and show irritable or aggressive outbursts following over-stimulation. They have language difficulties, and are poor with short-term memory skills and sequential processing.

Meningitis. Inflammation of the linings of the brain caused by a bacterial or viral infection. It can cause deafness, brain damage and epilepsy and marked changes in behaviour which include temper tantrums, aggression and mood swings.

Pervasive Developmental Disorder (PDD). Describes the whole spectrum of autism and atypical autistic disorders. (DSM-111R American Psychiatric Association.)

Phenylketonuria (PKU). An inherited metabolic disorder. An enzyme block results in phenylalanine accumulating in the body tissues which affects the brain and causes retardation.

Psychogenic. Where the causes of a psychiatric or psychological disorder are related to genetic factors, eg family medical history.

Rett's Syndrome. A regressive disorder which affects females. Around the age of 2 there is a deterioration in speech and the child becomes withdrawn. Other features of the disorder are hand clapping or wringing and seizures are common. Physical deterioration can occur due to muscle wasting.

Rubella. Infection during pregnancy which can result in deafness, blindness and mental retardation.

Semantic-Pragmatic Disorder. The diagnosis is generally given to children with normal or above average intelligence. There are severe receptive deficits with poor conversational skills and inappropriate use of language. The cognitive profile is the same as those with higher functioning autism as there will be difficulties with social interaction, restricted interests and imaginative play.

Tuberous Sclerosis. A complex genetic disorder which causes swellings of an organ or tissue. This affects brain function and behaviours typical of those with autism. There is little or no speech, ritualistic behaviours and overactivity. A high proportion of people with tuberous sclerosis will have epilepsy.

References and Further Reading

X Aarons, M and Gittens, T (1992) *The Handbook of Autism, A Guide for Parents and Professionals*, Routledge: London and New York.

Asperger, H (1944) as quoted in Wing, L (1976) *Early Childhood Autism*, (2nd edn), Pergamon Press: Oxford.

August, G, Stewart, M and Tsai, L (1983) The incidence of cognitive disabilities in the siblings of autistic children, *British Journal of Psychiatry*, 138, pp.416-422.

Baron-Cohen, S, Leslie, A M and Frith, U (1985) as quoted in Frith, U (1989) *Autism: Explaining the Enigma*, pp.156-174, Blackwell: Oxford.

Baron-Cohen, S (1989) Perceptual role taking and protodeclaritive pointing in autism, *British Journal of Developmental Psychology*, 7, pp.113-127.

Berard, G (1993) *Hearing Equals Behaviour*, Keats Publishing Inc. Connecticut.

Bettelheim, B (1967) as quoted in Rutter, M and Howlin, P, *Treatment of Autistic Children* (1987), Wiley and Sons: Chichester.

Christie, P (1990) *Education in a School for Autistic Children*, paper.

Department for Education (1994) *Code of Practice on the Identification and Assessment of Special Educational Needs*, DfEE.

Department for Education and Employment (1997) *The SENCO Guide*, DfEE.

Edwards, D (1991) The Efficacy of Daily Life Therapy at the Boston Higashi School, in *Therapeutic Approaches to Autism: Research and Practice*, collected papers from the conference organised by the Autism Research Unit.

Falvey, M (1995) *Inclusive and Heterogeneous Schooling*, Paul H Brookes Publishing Company, Baltimore: London.

Feuerstein, R et al (1991) *Mediated Learning Experience. Theoretical, Psychosocial and Learning Implications*, Freund Publishing House Ltd: England.

Folstein, S and Rutter, M (1977) Infantile Autism: A genetic study of 21 twin pairs, in *Journal of Child Psychology and Psychiatry*, 18, pp.297-321.

Frith, U (1989) *Autism: Explaining the Engima*, Blackwell: Oxford.

Frith, U (ed.) (1991) *Autism and Asperger Syndrome*, Cambridge University Press: Cambridge.

Gillberg, C, Johansson, M, Steffenburg, S, Berlin, O (1997) Auditory Integration Training in Children with Autism, in *Autism - The International Journal of Research and Practice*, Vol 1, No 1, Sage Publications.

Howlin, P and Rutter, M (1987) *Treatment of Autisic Children*, Wiley and Sons: Chichester.

Howlin, P (1988) Living with Impairment: The effects of children of having an autistic sibling, in *Child: Care, Health and Development*, No 14, pp.395-408.

Jordan, R and Powell, S (1995) *Understanding and Teaching Children with Autism*, Wiley and Sons: Chichester.

Jordan, R and Powell, S (1990) *The Special Curricular Needs of Autistic Children: Language and Thinking Skills*, The Association Heads and Teachers of Adults and Children with Autism: London.

Jordan, R (ed.) (1990) *The National Curriculum, Access for Pupils with Autism*, The Inge Wakehurst Trust: London.

Jordan, R (1991) Two Conflicting Therapies? The Option Method and Behaviourism as Treatments for the Fundamental Difficulties of Autism, in *Therapeutic Approaches to Autism: Research and Practice*, collected papers from the conference organised by the Autism Research Unit: Sunderland.

Kanner, L (1943) as quoted in Wing, L (1976) *Early Childhood Autism*, (2nd edn), Pergamon Press: Oxford.

Kaufman, B N (1994) *Son-Rise: The Miracle Continues*, H. J. Kramer Inc: Tiburon, California.

LaVigna, G (1987) Non-Aversive Strategies for Managing Behavior Problems, in *Handbook of Autism and Pervasive Developmental Disorders*, ed. Cohen, D and Donnellan, A. Wiley and Sons, Inc. and J. H. Winston and Sons: Maryland.

Leslie, A M (1987) as quoted in Frith, U *Autism: Explaining the Enigma*, pp.156-174, Blackwell: Oxford.

Lotter, V (1974) Factors related to outcome in autistic children, *Journal of Autism and Childhood Schizophrenia*, 4, pp.263-277.

Maurice, C (ed.) (1996) *Behavioral Intervention for Young Children with Autism*, PRO-ED Inc.

McGee, J (1998) *Gentle Teaching*, BT Internet. gentle@knoware.nl.

Mesibov, G (1997) Formal and Informal Measures on the Effectiveness of the TEACCH Programme, in *Autism - The International Journal of Research and Practice*, Vol 1, No 1, Sage Publications.

Mesibov, G (1986) *A Comprehensive Program for Serving People with Autism and their Families: The TEACCH Model*, paper.

National Autistic Society (1995) *Could This Be Autism?* London.

National Autistic Society (1994) *Approaches to Autism*. London.

Nind, M and Hewett, D (1994) *Access to Communication*, David Fulton Publishers: London.

O'Reilly, B (1991) Enzyme and Sulphur Oxidation Deficiencies in Autistic Children with Known Food/Chemical Intolerances, in *Therapeutic Approaches to Autism: Research and Practice*, collected papers from the conference organised by the Autism Research Unit: Sunderland.

Powell, S and Jordan, R (1997) *Autism and Learning*, Fulton Publishers: London.

Prior, M and Cummins, R (1992) Questions about Facilitated Communication, in *Journal of Autism and Developmental Disorders*, Vol 22, No 3, Plenum Press: New York.

Reichelt, K L, Scott, H, Knivesberg, A M, Wiig, K, Lind, G and Nodland, M (1990) as quoted in Shattock, P, *Proteins, Peptides and Problems in Autism*, paper.

Rimland, B (1993) High dosage vitamin B6 and magnesium therapy for autism and related disorders, paper 39E. Autism Research Institute, San Diego.

Rimland, B (1994) *Autism Research Review International*, Vol 8, No 2, Autism Research Institute, San Diego.

Rutter, M (1971, 1972, 1978 and 1979) in Howlin, P and Rutter, M, *Treatment of Autistic Children*, pp.10-21, Wiley and Sons: Chichester.

Rutter, M and Schopler, E (eds.) (1978) *Autism: a reappraisal of concepts and treatment*, Plenum Press: New York.

Schopler, E and Mesibov, G (eds.) (1988) *Diagnosis and Assessment in Autism*, Plenum Press: New York.

Shattock, P (1991) Proteins, Peptides and Problems in Autism, in *Therapeutic Approaches to Autism: Research and Practice*, collected papers from the conference organised by the Autism Research Unit.

Shattock, P and Savery, D (1997) *Autism as a Metabolic Disorder*, Autism Research Unit, University of Sunderland, UK.

Sherborne, V (1990) *Developmental Movement for Children*, Cambridge University Press: Cambridge.

Sussex Autistic Society (1997) *Members Survey*.

The Association of Headteachers of Autistic Children and Adults (1985) *The Special Curricular Needs of Autistic Children*, London.

Waring, R H (1991) as quoted in O'Reilly, B, *Enzyme and Sulphur Oxidation Deficiencies in Autistic Children with Known Food/Chemical Intolerances*, paper.

Warren, B (ed.) (1984) *Using the Creative Arts in Therapy*, Routledge: London.

Wing, L (ed.) (1976) *Early Childhood Autism* (2nd edn), Pergamon Press Ltd.: Oxford.

Wing, L and Gould, J (1979) 'Severe Impairments of Social Interaction and Associated Abnormalities in Children; Epidemiology and Classification'. *Journal of Autism and Developmental Disorders*, 9.1.

Wing, L (1996) *The Autistic Spectrum: A Guide for Parents and Professionals*, Constable Publishers: London.